Bicknell's Village Builder and Supplement.

Bicknell's Village Builder

A Victorian Architectural Guidebook

With a new introduction & commentary by
PAUL GOELDNER

Published for The Athenæum Library of Nineteenth Century America by
THE AMERICAN LIFE FOUNDATION & STUDY INSTITUTE

Watkins Glen, New-York

1976

The Athenæum Library of Nineteenth Century America is co-published by The Athenæum of Philadelphia and The American Life Foundation; every volume in this series, therefore, bears two ISBNs:

The American Life Foundation
ISBN : 0-89257-002-4

The Athenæum of Philadelphia
ISBN : 0-916530-02-7

Production notes: This new edition was supervised by Walnut Grove Graphic Design & Production Associates in Watkins Glen, New York. New composition of text and display as well as reproduction proofs of same was provided by Tier Oldstyle Typesetting in Binghamton, New York. Printing and binding was done at Valley Offset, Incorporated in Deposit, New York. The text paper is *Finch Opaque* seventy pound weight in a smooth finish. The cover stock of paperback copies is either Weyerhæuser *Andorra* or Strathmore *Rhododendron*. Hardback copies are bound in Holliston *Roxite-C* with endpapers of International *Springhill Index* and dustjackets of *Mead Offset Enamel*.

New Introduction & Commentary

—··—

Paul Goeldner

New Introduction & Commentary

Only a few years separate the publication of Bicknell's *Village Builder* in New York and Lewis Carroll's *Alice's Adventures in Wonderland* and *Through the Looking Glass* in England. In the intervening century the practical, cost-conscious world of American construction around 1870 has become as inaccessible to us as Alice's rabbit hole, while the fictional Alice, reincarnated in new editions, new illustrations, films and music, has become increasingly real. Although it no longer fulfills its original function, by reflecting a broad and detailed picture of a world our ancestors inhabited, Bicknell's looking glass may serve us better than it served them.

By many criteria Bicknell produced a mediocrity—unbalanced and arbitrary in its selection of projects, inconsistent in their presentation, and neglectful of those individuals, buildings and cities which a century of sifting tells us were significant and influential. But it is precisely because it neglects the superior architectural achievements that it conveys the broader patterns of taste. In title and content the book appeals to small communities. Even if we have never been to Ballston Spa or Bay City, we have seen similar houses, store fronts, and courthouses in towns we do know; and we assume, justly, that they were once ubiquitous.

It is not entirely clear to whom Bicknell addressed his publications nor how he assembled his material. The geographic spread of the inclusions indicates his ambition to market the book nationally, not a personal familiarity with the world beyond Elizabeth, New Jersey. (To him, Kansas City represented the "south west.") Phenomenal growth in the Midwest explains why most of the executed projects in the book are midwestern. Nothing in the designs or estimates suggests regionalism, however; and, if the addresses of Tennessee, New York, Illinois and Wyoming projects were scrambled, we would have no clues to put things right.

Superficial travelers have long cursed the Midwest as an undifferentiated vastness. Subtleties of terrain and climate were overwhelmed by an almost simultaneous burst of its agricultural and urban development after 1850. Without the historic variety of the East or the scenic variety of the West, the heartland has been identified by the homogeneity of the manmade environment. Its egalitarian abundance has attracted few scholars, but quantitatively the Midwest is probably unsurpassed as a place to study Victorian architecture.

A sameness in America's architectural character, often attributed to fast food franchises and motel chains, is already evident in the 1870s. To understand it best we should examine the advertisements. Ventilators, shutters, railings, plasterboard, mantels, roofing slates, and floor tiles were machine produced to be transported across oceans and continents. Earlier pattern books had disseminated design ideas which were subject to adaptation in execution; but, with the prefabrication of ornament, architecture became increasingly an art of assemblage.

A "practical work on architecture" appearing in 1870 came just before American architectural education and the American Institute of Architects had attained sufficient stature to define professionalism in terms which the public could understand and accept. No laws yet regulated the practice of architecture nor the use of the title "architect." Like Napoleon, who crowned himself, builders, carpenters, construction superintendents, and draftsmen became architects by identifying themselves as architects. Although our biographical information about the contributors to the *Village Builder* is fragmentary and uneven, we know that they represent as broad a range of architectural competence as of geographic distribution.

Since neither designers nor clients had formal training in architectural history, their stylistic terminology was rarely precise. But labels are unnecessary to those who know what they like and can point to an example in a book or a building. Most of the designs were not given any stylistic identification. Mansard or French roofs were fashionable in the East and St. Louis; their popularity in the Midwest and Texas continued well into the 1880s. The brackets, quoins, and low-pitched roofs of the Italianate mode are common to much of Elijah Myers's work though he didn't use the term in describing them. Surprisingly, the word "Baroque" is seldom applied to the swelling curves and generous ornament which characterize so much Victorian design. Other styles named by contributors to the *Village Builder* include Elizabethan, Gothic and Romanesque.

Practicality is exemplified in the cost estimates which accompany most of the designs. While it may seem odd that a $750 house appears in the same volume with a $5000 stable and an outrageously expensive courthouse, a psychology was employed which is similar to that of modern catalogues which juxtapose three-dollar handkerchiefs with "his and hers" airplanes. The simplest design may gain glamor by association with the expensive and elegant. The general pattern of the book is to begin with the "cheap," the residential, the "might be built" and work toward the "first class" and institutional buildings actually constructed for identified clients.

Probably the simpler designs were built many times in many communities and modified and adapted in many ways. They must have been the major selling point of the book. The *Supplement* is made up entirely of residential designs and details. Model specifications and contract forms complement three of the plans for small houses.

Floor Plans

Studying the floor plans of cottages and mansions helps us to describe the life styles of 1870. Parlors suggest formal elegance, and only the smallest house shows a living room instead. Some of the larger houses had both double parlors and less formal sitting rooms. A few of the small houses without dining rooms would have required their occupants to eat in the kitchen. Closets had become common for major bedrooms. There were also china closets and pantries in some designs; but built-in storage was generally limited. Those houses with libraries show no indication of shelving. Within the simple rectangles of the rooms one must imagine armoires, sideboards, and bookcases of generous proportions. Kitchens look incredibly bare without counters, sinks, or stoves shown on the plans.

Designs for larger residences generally show rooms for servants; but smaller houses obviously were intended for servant-less families. Some architects identify large sleeping rooms as chambers and smaller ones as bedrooms; this suggests that bedrooms were for the less influential members of the household: children and servants. Guests rooms, like parlors and exuberant exterior ornamentation, indicate a willingness to expend a significant fraction of a building and decorating budget on making an impression. However, a home can be a social center as well as a retreat. With or without servants our ancestors were hospitable, dispensing conversation and food as rich as their architectural ornament.

Mechanical Systems

The mechanical systems which were to revolutionize all architecture were in their infancy in 1870. Some of the houses still had fireplaces with coal grates; others made provision for stoves. A central heating system is described in the advertisement of Tuttle and Bailey who, 116 years later, are still manufacturing ventilators and registers. Bedrooms often received only borrowed heat through registers in the ceilings of rooms below. This, and a fear of night air, may explain why they often had only a single, small window.

Some of the house plans show no indoor plumbing. Others show bathtubs only. Kitchen sinks seem even more rare than bathtubs. Where toilets were indoors, habit or mistrust of their design sometimes located them near the back door. Earth closets, advertised by the Wakefield Earth Closet Company, were probably more practical and sanitary than water closets until it was possible to link household drains to an urban sewage system.

Gas light was specified because incandescent electric illumination was not even anticipated. Rural dwellings were still dependent on kerosene lamps. The telephone had not been invented.

Although without mechanical conveniences the house of 1870 was often more spacious and gracious than the house of 1970. In philosophy, location and every decorative line the village porch is the antithesis of the suburban deck or patio. Stables represent not only the architectural harmony of houses and outbuildings but an emotional bond between men and horses which cannot be successfully transferred to internal combustion engines.

Civic Buildings

Storefronts of 1870 exemplify the availability of large sizes of glass. Even so, hardly any have survived the 20th century urge to modernize with even larger show windows. Although the architects' drawings show no signs, we can be sure that photographs would have told a different story. A storekeeper, then as now, felt the need to identify his business.

The proliferation of schools was an obvious sign of progress in the late 19th century. Also progressive were the arrangements of wardrobes and the patented systems of ventilation in new school buildings. Assembly halls and chapels were probably more multipurpose than their names suggest. Special purpose laboratories and facilities for physical education were fashions of a later generation.

As befits an institution with a timeless message, the churches of the 1870s seem familiar to us. None of the designs are specifically denominational. To the extent that the elevations imitate high church traditions, the plans demonstrate low church functions. While there are modest provisions for Sunday school or committee rooms, the aberrations of the Akron plan had not yet been popularized.

Two courthouses represent the highest architectural aspirations of their communities. No other building type in their time and region was so socially and architecturally dominant. Sectarian Christianity was sometimes divisive but civil government in a proud democracy unified the citizens. The courthouse tower or dome identified the "Temple of Justice" as the heart of the county seat town like the church in the villages of medieval Europe or French Canada.

THE ARCHITECTS

The architects represented in the *Village Builder* are an interesting diversity of competence, naïveté, ambition, and amateurism. Did Bicknell assemble them by appeals to their vanity, by the promise of modest payment, or by the hope that publicity would attract to them an expanding clientele? Only three years passed between the original publication and the revised edition. In that short time at least one of the architects had moved his practice to a new state and another had started a new career in another field.

Although the architect of the cheap frame cottages in Plate 1 is not identified, he could have worked in the office of one of Bicknell's colleagues in Elizabeth whose designs dominate the *Supplement*. Although their ornament and form give charm to the cottages as two-dimensional drawings, they were indeed cheap and might well have appealed to speculative developers in industrial towns. The three-room plan has no windows on either side which would have encouraged its use on narrow lots.

Lyman Underwood

Lyman Underwood is represented in both the book (Plates 2, 2B) and the *Supplement* (Plate 5) with similar French cottages, so called because of their French or mansard roofs. Each was estimated to cost less than $4000 when of wood, clapboarded construction. The outline specification which accompanies Plate 2 refers to an unpublished cellar plan leading us quickly to an understanding that none of the designs in this publication could be constructed without more information than the plates provide. The specifications include very complete descriptions of the bathroom fixtures including silver-plated fittings for the washbowl.

Underwood, whose office was in Boston, also contributed a church design (Plate 42) which, "under favorable circumstances . . . might be built of stone for about $18,000." Although the façade incorporates Gothic details, the structural logic of Gothic design is totally absent; plan and elevation appear incompatible and unbuildable. Without redesign, it could probably not have been built at any price.

Brown & Grable

Brown and Grable of St. Louis submitted a brick cottage (Plates 3 and 4) and a French mansard dwelling (Plates 16 and 17) as well as specifications for building a similar cottage and a contract form for another house. The contract indicates that Alfred Grable was the partner who was the designer.

By our standards the cottage is comfortably designed. Grable was sensitive to the advantages of cross ventilation which must have been indispensable in a St. Louis summer. (It is said that British consuls there were given hardship pay because the tropical climate necessitated sending one's family to the mountains for the summer.) Unlike some of the designs in the book, the cottage could be built as drawn, which suggests that it may be a real building. It is only slightly confusing that the second floor plan is oriented to agree with the side elevation rather than the first floor plan. A graphic scale on the drawings disagrees with the scale given in the description; the drawings are right. Ornamental detail is appropriately scaled; its only flaw is that it was no longer in fashion.

On the other hand, the stylish French mansard dwelling is pompous. The front porch, even if accessible through the parlor window, is obviously a meaningless extravagance. Similarly, the cavernous stair hall gains a minimal result at a maximal cost.

Eugene R. Francisco

Plate 5, a two-story Italian cottage, is the only design which represents *Eugene R. Francisco* of Kansas City. In 1869 when most of the designs in the *Village Builder* were prepared, E. R. and John Francisco were associated as architects with an office in downtown Kansas City. The ease with which men then entered the professional was matched only by the ease with which they left it. By 1871 Eugene had become a cashier for a railroad and two years later his brother was in partnership as a carpenter.

The Italian cottage is characterized by unusually wide roof overhangs with heavy pendants at the corners. A small house without plumbing, it is among the most modestly estimated designs at $2000. Although the elevations show curtained basement windows there is no clear indication of stairs down from the first floor. And did Francisco really intend that shallow closet in front of a dining room window?

C. Edward Loth

C. Edward Loth crammed designs for two houses into Plate 6. As a technician he was probably very competent; his treatise, *Loth's Practical Stair Builder*, is advertised as another Bicknell publication. His inadequacies as a designer are evident in awkward planning. The bedroom in his one-story cottage open only from the kitchen and are each smaller than the linen closet of his two-story house.

Edgar Berryman

Edgar Berryman, a Buffalo architect, has left no biographical record, but his design for a Gothic cottage (Plates 7, 8 and 9) indicates some sophistication. There is an element of urbane humor in calling a mansion a cottage; in everything but name the house is quite pretentious. Its principal claims to gothicism are the lofty roof line and the cusped window frames which are vaguely Tudor in inspiration but skimpy in scale if executed in wood. Because the kitchen and dining room are connected only by a serving window between pantry and china closet, the functioning of the household would be dependent on servants. Separation of employer and domestic staff is not consistent, however, because there are no back stairs to the servants' bed rooms over the kitchen. Obviously expensive, this is one of the few designs without a cost estimate.

Alexander Campbell Bruce

The cottage villa in Plates 10, 11, and 12 is interesting as an early work of *A. C. Bruce* for a Tennessee political and industrial leader, Colonel Arthur St. Clair Colyar. Both architect and client were long-lived and had significant careers. Colyar (1818-1907), a lawyer by profession, a debater by choice, and a member of a prominent pioneer family, had all the credentials for political success. A businessman by instinct, he consistently counseled moderation in a turbulent, extravagant era. Though opposed to secession, he bowed to the will of his native state and was serving in the Confederate Congress at the end of the Civil War. After returning to Winchester, Tennessee, he soon controlled the Sewanee Mining Company, renamed the Tennessee Coal and Railroad Company, which through his astute business management and his political activity on its behalf grew to a major industrial firm.

Colyar's interest in the Sewanee area east of Winchester was related to more than its coal mines. He had been foremost in assembling the 9500-acre campus there for the University of the South. But if the Bruce-designed villa was built in the Sewanee area it could have been only a part-time residence for Col. Colyar and his large family who were increasingly tied to the political scene in Nashville where they had moved in 1866. A rural setting with plentiful servants would explain the lack of plumbing and modest cost of the villa. Its irregular plan was well adapted to "large and well ventilated" rooms, although the second floor bedrooms each have but a single window.

Alexander Campbell Bruce (1835-1927), the architect, prepared drawings as professional as may be found in Bicknell's book. He is among the few contributors who drew stairs to indicate with dotted lines their rising above the level of the first floor plan. (Modern drawings would break off the stair without showing the full run.) Bruce, who had lived in Nashville from the age of 12, had been trained there by an English architect, H. M. Ackeroyd. By 1871 he had his own practice in Knoxville. His professional career was advanced by a move to Atlanta in 1879 where he was active in the firm of Bruce and Morgan from 1882 to 1904. He was made a Fellow in the American Institute of Architects in 1889. Extant works of his firm include multi-story office structures such as the Prudential and Empire buildings in downtown Atlanta, several large churches and the 1888 administration building of the Georgia Institute of Technology.

G. B. Croff

Although *G. B. Croff*'s "Design for a Cheap Residence with French Roof" (Plates 13 and 14) was built for a bank cashier in Ballston Spa, New York, its plan shows walls so thin they appear inadequate to support the ornament. Unless one of the plates is reversed (mirror image) the second floor will not relate to the first. The elevations are more believable. If these particular façades no longer exist, there are many similar ones which do. Croff also designed the two store fronts in Plate 34 which are identified as having been constructed in his home town, Fort Edward, and in Ballston Spa. They exemplify the limitless combinations of machine produced Victorian ornament.

Elijah E. Myers

Elijah E. Myers is the architect who dominates the *Village Builder* with 18 plates and seven of the 17 projects actually built for identified clients. Although his fame has faded, he was busy from Virginia to Idaho in the 1880s designing major public buildings. Three of the state capitols he designed are still in use, those of Michigan, Texas and Colorado. A smaller capitol for Idaho was replaced in 1912. His city halls in Grand Rapids and Richmond were subjects of major preservation campaigns in the 1960s—only the Richmond example survived. He was the architect of large hospitals in Michigan and Illinois. Although H. H. Richardson won the competition to design the Allegheny County Buildings in Pittsburgh, Myers, who had had more experience designing courthouses, was among the four other architects invited to compete.

Myers learned his profession in Philadelphia where he was born in 1832. He opened his own architectural office in Springfield, Illinois shortly after the Civil War. In 1872, after winning the competition to design the Michigan capitol, he moved to Detroit where he died in 1909. Although the Springfield years were brief, they were the foundation of his career and are uniquely illuminated for us by his contributions in the *Village Builder*.

Plates 15, 18, and 19 present two suburban residences, the first a speculative design and the second actually built for a client in Springfield. Although comparable in number and use of rooms, the second is somewhat larger and more richly ornamented. It is charateristic of Myers to estimate the unbuilt project at $4,500 and the completed one at $10,000. Throughout his career he underestimated costs. Often his clients doubled their construction budgets but occasionally they dismissed him as soon as the contractors had submitted their bids.

A much larger residence, the Lewis Thomas farm house (Plates 23-26) was built in Montgomery County, Illinois for $30,000. Here, as in one of his suburban residences, Myers's plans show a family room, a term none of his contemporaries used and one not popularized until after 1950. The farm house also has a family bed room, part of a two-room suite isolated from guests and hired help. Particularly suited to a farm environment is the large dining room, accessible to field hands directly from porches on both sides and open to, though clearly separate from, the kitchen. While employer, family and employees probably ate most meals together, the family room was probably meant on some occasions to be a family dining room. All of Myers's house designs show uncertainty in where to locate a bathroom, but the Thomas house raises the question of whether the design could actually have been constructed as shown. It is reached only through a bedroom, and, although shown at the same level in plan, it is in a wing six steps lower. Did the piping run through the dining room below or was water carried up and back in buckets as must have been done in the servants' bath? The location of the water closets shows how minimally they were brought indoors. This example is a rare link in an evolutionary process. It indicates a hesitancy to trust new technology and a common reluctance of clients to accept possibilities and conveniences which will markedly modify their behavior patterns.

All three of Myers's residential designs are Italianate with hip roofs, bracketed cornices and quoins. He used balustrades and arched openings where he could. The cable moulding around the front door of the Thomas farm house was a favorite detail in this phase of his career. The tower of the Thomas house is so important a part of the elevations that it is disappointing to see no stairway going up into it.

Myers's client, Lewis Thomas, was a pioneer farmer in Montgomery County whose farming methods and business ability were widely admired. He was a great advocate of farm groves or woodlots. Before the age of wire fencing, he hedged his fields with Osage Orange, a practice which brought him wide recognition which he turned to effect by promoting the alternative name, Bois d'arc (bow wood). He was even able in the years of the organization of Montgomery County to name his own jurisdiction Bois d'arc Township. The house Myers designed for him burned in 1888.

It is as difficult for us to comment on the merits of a carriage house and stable (Plate 32) as it would have been for Myers to analyze a gas station. It appears, however, to be too large and richly ornamented to be estimated at $2,700.

The Conkling Block in Springfield and the Ayers Block in Jacksonville, Illinois, represent commercial structures of a type easily found in the Midwest today although the stamped metal ornament does not always survive intact and the store fronts below the second floor have seldom escaped modernization. Dates on the building façades identify these as having been erected in 1869 and 1868.

Externally, Myers's frame schoolhouse (Plate 36) bears an unflattering resemblance to his brick carriage house and stable. The rich detailing of the gable and entrance are a bit unusual and make this a drawing we might enjoy seeing in a colored rendering. The internal arrangements are extremely simple. The cramped stair with its wedge-shaped treads seems by our standards to violate the most basic safety standards, particularly in non-fireproof construction.

If there is a single outstanding building in the *Village Builder*, it is Myers's Macoupin County Courthouse (Plates 45-48), "strictly the only fire-proof building in the country." If other structures illustrated in the book are still standing, they should be identified, but none can have a more interesting history nor be more worthy of a visit than this courthouse in Carlinville, Illinois.

In March 1867, a few weeks after the Illinois legislature authorized an expenditure of $50,000 for a new courthouse, the county court appointed four commissioners to erect the new building. They included Judge Thaddeus L. Loomis, who was authorized to enter contracts obligating the county, and George H. Holliday, the County Clerk, who recorded some of his and his colleagues' improprieties in one of the most flagrant examples of political graft in the Grant era. His beautiful handwriting may betray a fondness for "nice things" which tempted him to raid the public treasury for personal gain as well as to build an extravagant public monument.

Myers cannot have been totally innocent in the schemes which drove the ultimate cost of the courthouse to $1,342,-000. His fees alone totalled nearly $60,000 including $3,700 in travelling expenses and a $9,400 joint payment with Holliday. The escalation of costs began gradually but

accelerated markedly in 1869 after the legislature permitted issuance of bonds at ten per cent interest "to raise whatever sum may be necessary to complete said courthouse and improvements connected therewith." Only then did the commissioners vote themselves a five per cent commission. It was about that time, also, that Myers must have submitted the drawings to Bicknell with his comment, "The building throughout is of the finest and best material, no cost having been spared to make it perfect in all its parts."

The elevations show a curious attempt to draw the dome in perspective. As shown here the dome details are similar to those of the Arch Street Presbyterian Church in Philadelphia (1850-1855), a design of Joseph Hoxie which must have been familiar to Myers; as actually constructed the dome is more realistically depicted in the 1872 catalogue of the Philadelphia Architectural Iron Company. The courtroom and many of the external features of the courthouse reflect the influence of the Arch Street church, the Corinthian porticoes and the window details particularly. If the sculptural figures shown on the ridges above the pediments were ever installed, they and their pedestals have not survived; they were esthetically excessive and were probably never ordered. An improvement in the completed building are the stairs from the side entrances which were built with a short flight to a landing where they divide.

Those side entrances are no longer used; the transverse corridor shown on the first floor plan has been closed to create more office and storage space. The functions of some offices have changed but the heavy masonry walls were built to resist change. All of the stairs, doors, window sash and frames were fabricated of cast iron to assure a fireproof structure. Except for the change of the Judge's Private Room to a men's toilet, the second floor is much as the plan indicates. The dome is the major feature of the courtroom and once contained a $3000 bronze chandelier. An element of elegance which has disappeared is a rich color scheme now obscured on all the metalwork by a thick layer of gray paint.

Plates 52-54 show proof of Myers's mastery of another specialized building type, the jail. A custom which may yet survive in some counties enabled the sheriff to augment his income with payments for prisoners' meals prepared by the sheriff's wife. Convenience of this service and a need for continuous surveillance created the building type exemplified here, a jailor's residence, as cheerfully domestic as possible in juxtaposition with a grimly efficient cell block.

Elbridge Boyden & Son

A Worcester architectural firm, *Elbridge Boyden and Son*, designed the "first dwelling" of Mr. J. A. Hovey of Ballston Spa, the town which is better represented in Bicknell's *Village Builder* than any other American community. The Hovey House (Plates 20-22) was very large with nine bedrooms, a bath and a boudoir on the "chamber" plan. Each bedroom had least one closet; one had three. The inclusion of an office with separate entrance and the large service wing give an impression of a self-sufficient community or institution. The pantry (12 by 13 feet) is enormous. A construction detail indicates balloon-framed wood construction. The elevations show it embellished with quoins, pilasters, a bracketed cornice and heavily ornamented dormers in the patterned slate mansard roof.

Plates 30 and 31 illustrate a "first class stable" also designed by the Boydens and built in their own Worcester, Massachusetts. An extremely complex roof seems to be the identifying element of its "Elizabethan" character. Among the dramatic changes of the past century is the mechanization of personal transportation. This $5000 answer to a gentleman's parking problem certainly exemplifies that change.

F. Wm. Reader

F. Wm. Reader, a St. Louis architect, designed a suburban residence (Plates 27 and 28) which has an unreal, storybook quality. Probably the architect's dream house, it has an unusual dependence on mechanical equipment: a ducted hot air furnace, wash basins in every bedroom, and a dumbwaiter which provides the only connection between kitchen and dining room. The basement is divided into specialized work spaces, inconveniently related. The first floor is very formal, the parlor so aloof that it can be reached only through the library. The second floor has a large sewing room lighted by a generously glazed conservatory. The attic has six generous rooms and a stair to the roof. One can fantasize this house occupied by exiled central European nobility or by expensive ladies of easy virtue; but not by one's great grandparents in small midwestern towns.

C. Bolin Stark

Plate 29 illustrates a "cheap city dwelling" designed by C. Bolin Stark of Philadelphia. Somewhat out of place among the village and suburban villas, this row house is a vertical arrangement suited only to a bachelor or childless couple with very strong legs. Its narrow front limits the available area for ornament. Even so, at $2000 it would have been the bargain of the decade.

Theo. F. Ladue

Theo. F. Ladue, an architect in Lincoln, Illinois, designed a brick schoolhouse with mansard roof for that town (Plates 37 and 38). We seldom appreciate how the social pressures of general public education raised standards of personal cleanliness. In the transition era, when some children were still sewed into their underwear for the winter, there was an urgency in the improvement of school ventilation systems, several of which were patented. The elevation drawing shows two ornamental towerlets which functioned as exhausts for the foul air shafts of the Ruttan system.

Uniformity is often a result of applied science. Here, the ideal schoolroom and wardrobe is repeated identically ten times. The printed comments mention water closets in the basement, an almost essential convenience where great numbers of children were assembled in one building. The written description gives us a good idea of the color effects of the zebra-striped wainscots and the red brick exterior walls with cream-colored brick trim.

Cochrane & Piquenard

Although Cochrane and Piquenard are represented only by a modest wooden chapel in Cheyenne, Wyoming, they give Bicknell the distinction of including the architects of five extant state capitols in the Village Builder. In addition to the three designed by Elijah Myers, we can add those of Iowa and Illinois. Cochrane was very successful at winning commissions. Piquenard was a sensitive designer who moved to Springfield in 1870 to work out many of the details of the Illinois capitol and who spent the years 1871-1874 preparing the drawings for the Iowa capitol.

The chapel in Cheyenne (Plates 39-41) was a fashionably embellished and liturgically simplified version of the mission churches designed by Richard Upjohn in the previous decades. As a variation on a successful formula, it too is successful, but possibly less interesting than its designers.

John C. Cochrane (1833-1887) was born and educated in New Hampshire. At the age of 23 he began the practice of architecture in Davenport, Iowa, and after eight years there he moved to Chicago. His independent commissions included courthouses in Illinois, Indiana, Iowa and Missouri as well as many hospitals and churches.

Idealism and the improvement of society were seriously pursued in the 19th century as part of the American experiment. Emancipation, temperance, penal reform, literacy, and public health were among the many specific organized causes. There were also dozens of utopian experiments, communities attempting to follow patterns of social perfection. Alfred H. Piquenard devoted nearly a decade of his life to the Icarian movement of Etienne Cabet. Exiled in England, the French journalist was influenced by More's Utopia to write his own Voyage en Icarie, a work so popular that thousands of Frenchmen were clamoring for the establishment of a real Icaria in America. Piquenard was among the advance guard which sailed from LeHavre in February 1848 to establish Cabet's Nouvelle Icarie in Denton County, Texas. The first season was a nightmare of land fraud, crop failure, disease, and even madness for some; but Piquenard survived to greet Cabet who arrived in New Orleans the following winter. Learning of the availability of Nauvoo, the Illinois city evacuated by the Mormons, the Icarians started up the Mississippi by steamboat in March 1849. Piquenard was among the incorporators of the Icarian community at Nauvoo in February 1851.

In practice the experiment continued to be frustrating. Cabet was dictatorial; one visitor reported that jobs were assigned arbitrarily. An architect (Piquenard?) complained that he repaired shoes while a cobbler supervised building construction. Succumbing to factionalism the community was dissolved in 1856. Piquenard went to St. Louis where for a time he was associated in the architectural practice of George I. Barnett. Among his independent commissions was the Madison County Courthouse in Winterset, Iowa, which was under construction at the time of his death in 1876.

David S. Hopkins

We would like to know more about David S. Hopkins, the architect of a Romanesque church in Grand Rapids

(Plates 43 and 44). Because it was a substantial commission of 1868 or earlier and because Hopkins's name appears as a Grand Rapids architect in Michigan directories through 1883 or later, we may assume that he left other equally impressive evidences of his career.

Photographs of Grand Rapids in the late 19th century identify this church as the First Methodist or, because of its location at Division and Fountain Streets, the Division Street M. E. Church. Its cornerstone was laid May 16, 1868; the congregation moved into the basement on New Year's Day 1869; and the formal opening was the following June 23. Large as it was, Hopkins's design was always dwarfed by the Fountain Street Baptist Church in the next block. Around 1913 the Methodists acquired a less confining site on which to build and the 1869 church was demolished to make way for commercial development.

A noteworthy feature of this church as presented in the drawings is the formal, fixed seating in the basement level where we might expect a social hall adapted to church dinners. The best explanation in this instance is the vigor of the Sunday School movement; two classrooms with sliding doors open into the basement lecture room. However, there is a Methodist precedent which may have been unknown to the architect and congregation in Grand Rapids. John Wesley's own chapel in City Road in London has a large evening chapel and a smaller morning chapel adjacent.

In any public building of 100 years ago we are impressed with the functional importance of stairs. Many parishioners apparently thought nothing of climbing two long flights to sit in the gallery and even the old and lame had to climb one full story. While functionally advantageous, neither elevators nor single story planning lend themselves to the architectural treatments possible with stairs.

Cyrus Kinne Porter

Cyrus Kinne Porter's Bay County Courthouse in Bay City, Michigan (Plates 49-51) is far more typical than Myers's extravagant project in Carlinville. Its squared-domed tower would identify it as a courthouse to millions of Americans then and now. Even though the Bay City example was demolished in 1933, an almost identical example, concealed on one side by modern additions, exists in St. John, Michigan. There, in October 1869, the Clinton County Board of Supervisors voted to adopt a design like that in Bay County. They were assisted in that decision by the fact that the town of St. John, anxious to keep its county seat status, had already excavated the basement, completed the foundation and paid the architect (presumably Porter).

A perspective view of the Bay County Courthouse was used as the frontispiece in the *Village Builder*. Three dimensional drawings would have heightened our appreciation of other designs in the book. In this case they raise at least one question. Where did all those chimneys come from? The building is described as heated by steam, the elevations show a maximum of four chimneys, and we count at least seven in the perspective.

Cyrus K. Porter was born near Syracuse, New York, in 1828. His long career took him to Chicago; Brantford, Ontario; Buffalo; Bay City and back to Buffalo before his death there in 1910. The office in Bay City was never more than a branch of his Buffalo firm, but it must have been busy for a few years. Two sons were associated with Porter in the practice of architecture and continued the firm after his death.

Considering the importance of fraternal orders in the social life of the 19th century, it is a little surprising that no lodge halls are included in the *Village Builder*. A man of his times, Porter belonged not only to the Masonic and Odd Fellows lodges but was himself the founder of the Royal Templars of Temperance. The temperance cause was also represented by another fraternal association, the Sons of Temperance, with grand lodges in most states. Col. A. S. Colyar was proud to have joined the Sons of Temperance as a young boy and to have been an active member for more than 80 years. Bicknell's collection of architects and clients was a very limited sampling of American society. To have two of that select group so devoted to temperance tells us something about their era which we must take more seriously if we wish to understand them. Temperance represents virtue defined so that it can be conscientiously practiced and promoted. A hundred years later goodness seems somewhat more suspect and less popular.

Commentary on the Supplement

Bicknell's *Village Builder* was sold at ten dollars per copy. For two dollars more one could obtain the *Supplement* bound in the same volume. The *Supplement* includes twenty additional plates and designs for seventeen houses and a stable. Quantitatively, the *Supplement* was a real bargain. A few of the plates are anonymous, but more than half are the work of architects who were Bicknell's neighbors in Elizabeth: C. Graham and Son, D. B. Provoost, and T. Thompson. In their day, architects could advertise without violating any code of ethics. They each have advertisements in the book, but the supplement provides a showcase of their abilities.

Most of the residences in the *Supplement* are mansardic designs—some with sinuous contrasting concave and convex mansards. The Graham firm, like some other architects in a period of invention, had patented the design of an ornamental gable to be inset in a French roof. Did it sell? Probably not. The real merit of books of architectural designs is that after studying them well one can come up with a better idea.

Bicknell's
Village Builder
and
Supplement.

BAY COUNTY COURT HOUSE,

Bay City, Mich.

Lith. by J. Bien. 16 & 18 Park Place. NY

BICKNELL'S
VILLAGE BUILDER

ELEVATIONS AND PLANS

FOR

COTTAGES, VILLAS, SUBURBAN RESIDENCES, FARM HOUSES, STABLES AND
CARRIAGE HOUSES, STORE FRONTS, SCHOOL-HOUSES, CHURCHES,
COURT-HOUSES, AND A MODEL JAIL;

ALSO

EXTERIOR AND INTERIOR DETAILS FOR PUBLIC AND PRIVATE BUILDINGS,

WITH APPROVED FORMS OF CONTRACTS AND SPECIFICATIONS.

CONTAINING FIFTY-FIVE PLATES DRAWN TO SCALE;

SHOWING THE STYLE AND COST OF BUILDING IN DIFFERENT SECTIONS OF THE COUNTRY, BEING AN
ORIGINAL WORK,
COMPRISING THE DESIGNS OF FIFTEEN LEADING ARCHITECTS, REPRESENTING THE NEW ENGLAND,
MIDDLE, WESTERN AND SOUTH-WESTERN STATES.

REVISED EDITION.
WITH THREE ADDITIONAL PLATES AND A VARIETY OF DETAILS.

New York:
A. J. BICKNELL & CO.,
ARCHITECTURAL BOOK PUBLISHERS,
27 WARREN STREET.
1872.

Printed by the N. Y. Lithographing, Engraving, and Printing Co.,
16 & 18 Park Place, New York.

INTRODUCTION.

Several years experience in the sale of Architectural Books has taught us, that in bringing out a practical work on Architecture, it is necessary to include a great variety of styles of buildings; and in presenting this volume to the public, we feel assured that it is better adapted to the North, South, East and West, than any previous production of similar character.

Several well-known architects, whose names will be found in connection with the description of plates, have aided us in perfecting this work. It has been our object in the selection of designs principally to include buildings of moderate cost, although we have introduced several elaborate specimens, all of which are suggestive, and may be executed in a plainer way for one-half the given cost.

The estimates are made at the various localities where the designs have been prepared; including Boston, Worcester, Philadelphia, Buffalo, Chicago, St. Louis; Springfield and Lincoln, Ill.; Kansas City, Mo.; Nashville, Tenn.; and Fort Edward, N.Y.

The work is chiefly made up of elevations, plans and details of cottages, villas, and suburban houses; yet much attention has been given to model designs for churches, court-houses, and other public and private buildings.

The elevations are mostly drawn on a scale of one-eighth, one-twelfth, or one-sixteenth; the details on a scale of one-half to three-fourths of one inch to the foot; all of which can be easily comprehended and executed.

The demand for previous publications that we have brought to public notice is an evidence of the increasing want of such a work as the VILLAGE BUILDER, which is not characterized by the style of any one author or locality, but is general in its adaptation.

A. J. BICKNELL & CO.

FRONTISPIECE.

Perspective view of Bay County Court-house, Bay City, Mich. Plates 49, 50 and 51 show the front and side elevations, plans and details.

PLATE 1.

THREE DESIGNS FOR CHEAP FRAME COTTAGES.

Fig. 1. Front elevation of cottage with hip roof.

Fig. 2. First floor plan, containing three rooms and porch. This design can be built for $750.

Fig. 3. Elevation of cottage, suitable for plan of Fig. 1. Cost $1,000.

Fig. 4. Front elevation of cottage, containing six rooms.

Fig. 5. First floor plan of Fig. 4.

Fig. 6. Second floor plan of Fig. 4. Cost $1,200.

The designs on this plate are drawn on the scale of one-eighth of one inch to the foot.

Plate 1.

Fig. 1.

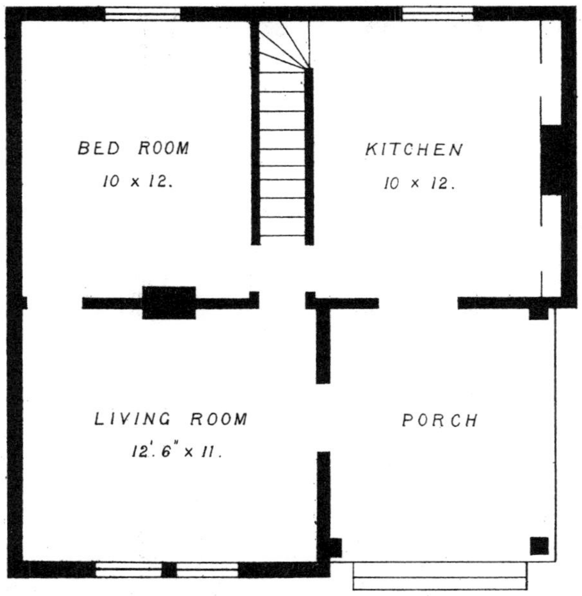

Fig. 2.

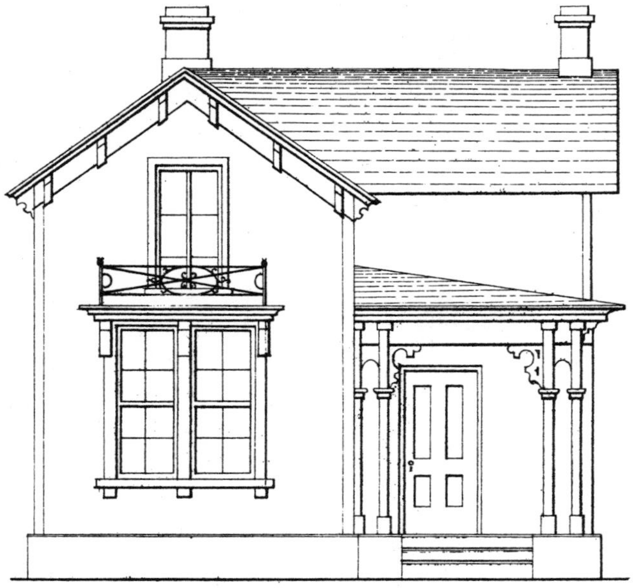

BED ROOM
10 × 12.

KITCHEN
10 × 12.

LIVING ROOM
12'. 6" × 11.

PORCH

Fig. 3.

Scale: ⅛ of 1 inch to the foot.

Fig. 4.

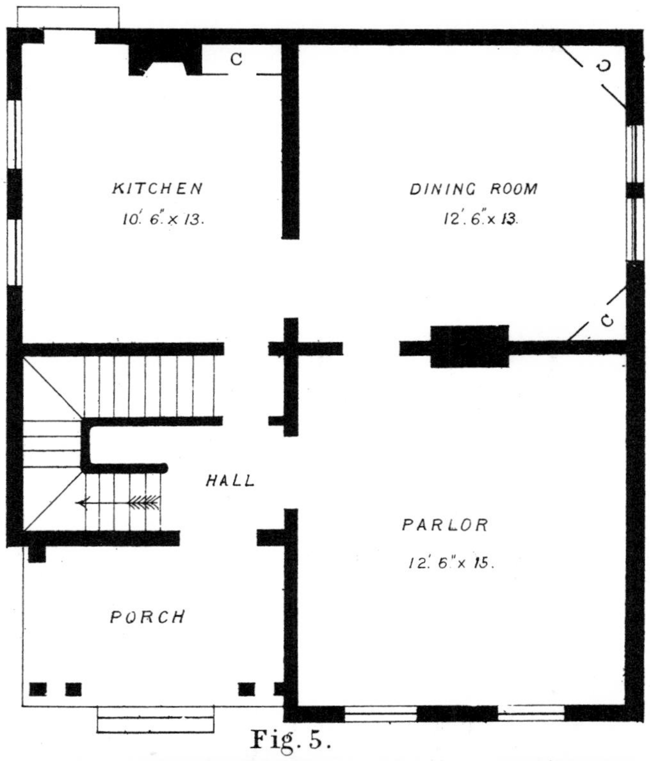

Fig. 5.

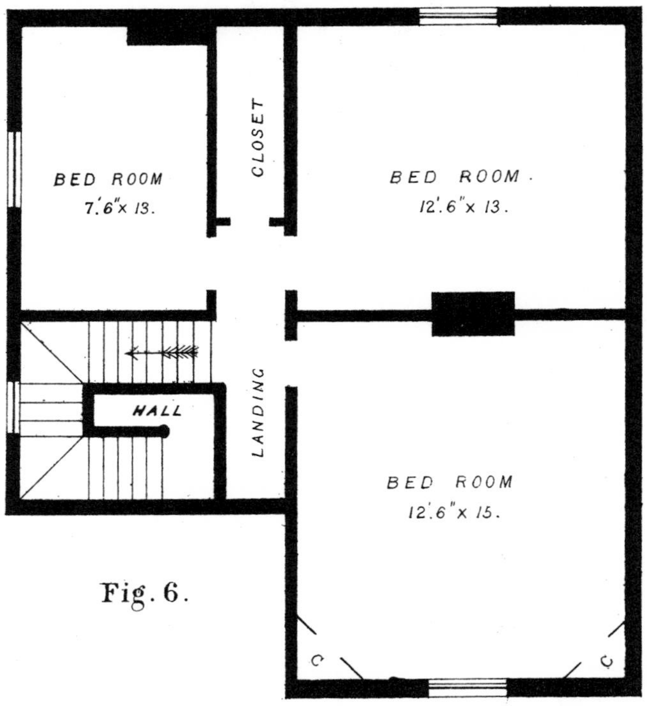

KITCHEN
10'. 6" × 13.

DINING ROOM
12'. 6" × 13.

HALL

PARLOR
12'. 6" × 15.

PORCH

Fig. 6.

BED ROOM
7'. 6" × 13.

CLOSET

BED ROOM
12'. 6" × 13.

LANDING

HALL

BED ROOM
12'. 6" × 15.

Lith by J. Bien 16 & 18 Park Place N.Y.

PLATE 2.

DESIGN FOR A FRENCH COTTAGE.

Lyman Underwood, Architect, 13 Exchange Street, Boston.

The front elevation and floor plans of this cottage are perhaps, sufficiently explicit. It is simply but conveniently arranged for a small family. It is intended to be built of wood, and painted to harmonize with the surroundings. The stories are ten and nine feet. The elevation is drawn to a scale of eight feet to one inch, and the floors sixteen feet to one inch. The cost under ordinary circumstances would be about $3,800.

Plate 2.

FRONT ELEVATION

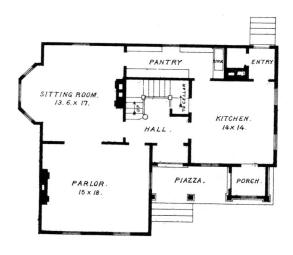

PLAN OF FIRST FLOOR.

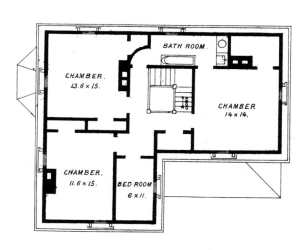

PLAN OF SECOND FLOOR.

Lith by J Bien 16 & 18 Park Place N.Y.

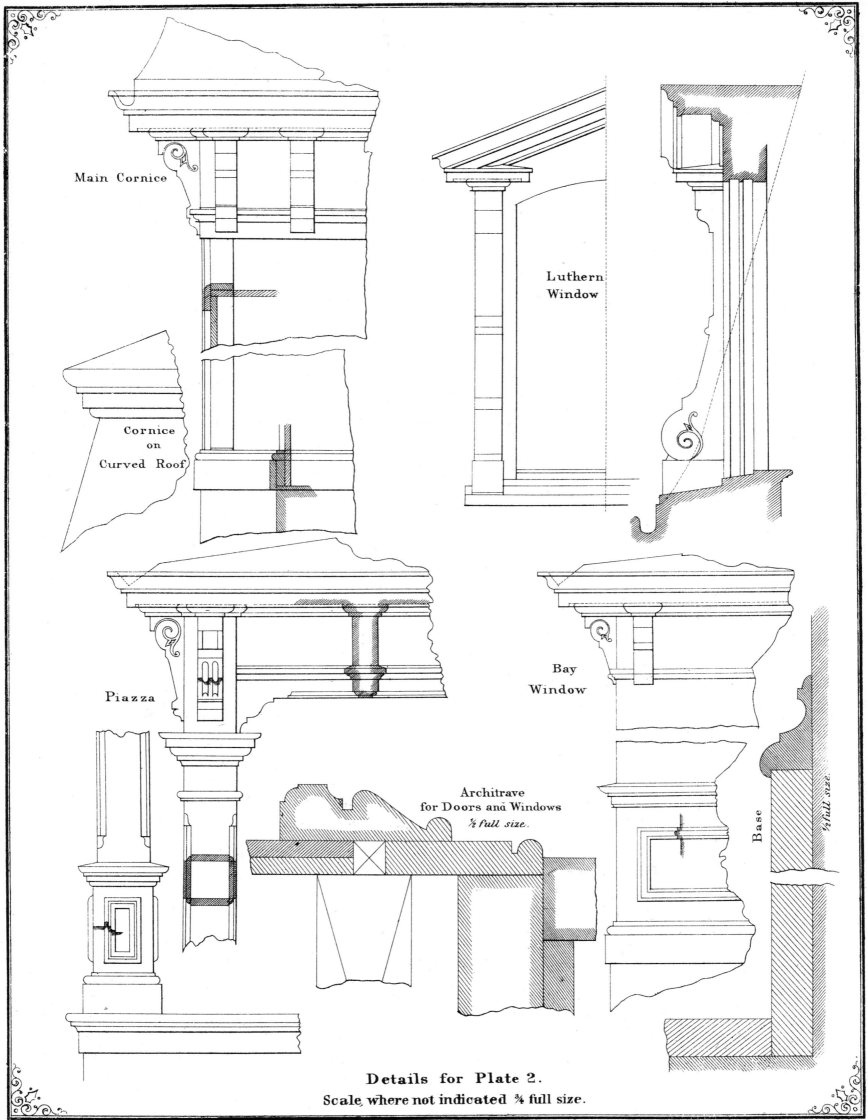

Plate 2.B.

Main Cornice

Luthern Window

Cornice on Curved Roof

Piazza

Bay Window

Architrave for Doors and Windows
½ full size.

Base

½ full size.

Details for Plate 2.
Scale where not indicated ¾ full size.

Lith by J. Bien 16 & 18 Park Place N.Y.

SPECIFICATIONS.

SPECIFICATIONS of the Materials to be Furnished and Labor to be Performed in the Erection and Completion of a Wooden Dwelling-House, according to a set of plans, shown on Plate 2, furnished by L. Underwood, Architect, 13 Exchange Street, Boston.

GENERAL DESCRIPTION.

The size of the house and the size and arrangement of all the rooms, etc., are to be as shown on the plans, which are to be considered as a part of this specification ; and which, with the writing and figures thereon, together with the detail drawings, are to be adhered to in every respect. The figures in all cases are to take the precedence of measurements on the plans.

EXCAVATION, STONE WORK, &c.

The contractor is to do all of the excavating for the cellar, drains and cistern, dig well, etc., and to put in the cellar and bulkhead walls, build foundations for piers and chimneys, and to do all the stonework necessary to receive the frame. The cellar and bulkhead walls are to be 18″ thick at the bottom and 14″ at the top, built with stone laid in cement mortar, and are to be carried up to the proper height to receive the sills. The cellar is to be 8′ 6″ deep in the clear of the joists. There is to be a dry well, 4′ in diameter at the bottom and 2′ 6″ at the top, and 6′ deep, built where shown on the plans. The walls are to be of stone laid dry, carried up to within 18″ of the top of the ground and covered with flagging stones. There is to be a 5″ vitrified earthenware drain-pipe from the waste-pipe to the sink, to the dry well, provided with a stench trap. The cellar wall above the grade is to be built of large stone, with an even face on the outside. The joints are to be well pointed and drawn. There is to be a well located as per plan, and bricked up with a 4′ wall of hard burned brick, laid in cement and is to be covered with flagging stones.

All earth that is excavated is to be deposited in such places in the lot as the proprietor may direct

BRICKWORK.

Piers are to be built, as shown on the cellar plan, with good hard burned brick, and carried up to the sills. The chimneys are to be built, as shown on the plans, of a good quality of chimney brick, and to be topped out with good hard burned brick of uniform color, according to designs given in the elevations. All of the flues are to be fastened throughout on the inside. There are to be funnel irons, of such sizes as may be directed, put in the chimneys, so that stoves may be put up in all the rooms.

There is to be a rain-water cistern, as shown on the plans, of 2,500 gallons capacity, built in the usual manner, with hard burned bricks laid in cement, and is to be thoroughly cemented on the inside, and provided with a flagging stone cover and a vitrified earthen overflow pipe connected with the drain running to the dry well. The overflow pipe is to have a bend-trap.

CARPENTERS' WORK.

The frame is to be made and set up in a good and workmanlike manner, with good, sound, square-edged spruce timbers and joists of such sizes as are marked on the plans. The floor joists are to be bridged with truss bridging. The walls and roof to be boarded with sound pine boards, mill-planed and matched ; to be well laid and nailed. The roofs are to be prepared for slating or tinning, as may be required. The outside finish is to be well wrought and put up according to the detail drawings, and is to be of sound, seasoned pine lumber, free from knots, sap or shakes. The walls of the house are to be clapboarded with Eastern pine clapboards, planed to an even thickness and moulded, and laid so as to lap not less than 1½″, and all to be thoroughly nailed.

All projections, mitre-joints, and other exposed places are to be well leaded with sheet lead so as to prevent all leakage.

SLATING AND TINNING.

All the roofs are to be slated with good Pennsylvania slates of uniform color, laid on tarred sheathing paper, and secured with Swedes iron nails. The slates on the Mansard roofs are to be 8″ × 12″, with the lower ends rounded.

The roofs of the Bay and Luthern windows, and of the piazza, are to be tinned with the best quality of roofing tin, put on with soldered joints. The chimneys and all other places liable to leak are to be secured with lead or zinc and made perfectly tight.

The gutters to the main roof are to be of wood and formed as shown on the details of cornice, and to have lead eaves pipes, and two 3″ (inside measurement) round wooden conductors put up where directed. The gutters for piazza and bay window are also to be of wood, with 2″ wooden conductors. As many of the conductors are to connect with the cistern as may be directed. All others are to have proper turnouts at the bottom.

WINDOWS.

The window-frames are to be made according to the detail drawings, with Southern hard pine, pulley stiles and parting beads. The pockets for the weights are to be cut into the pulley stiles and secured with screws. The sashes are to be of pine 1¾″ thick, and double hung with weights, best hemp sash cord, and 1¾″ axle pulleys, and to be provided with good bronzed sash fastenings. The stop-beads are to be of soft pine, and are to be secured with round-headed blued iron screws.

The cellar windows are to have plank frames made in the usual manner, and the sashes to be hung so as to swing up under the first floor. The glass is to be of such sizes as are figured on the plans.

There are to be outside blinds on all the windows, to be hung with wrought-iron hinges and secured with good substantial fastenings.

PARTITIONS AND FURRINGS.

All partitions are to be set with 2″ × 3″ joists, placed 16″ from centers and bridged. All are to be of even widths, and to be set straight and true. The cappings to the hall partitions are to be 3″ × 4″. All the partition joists, when practicable, are to go through the floor and stand on the partition cap below.

All ceilings are to be furred with 1″ × 3″ strips, placed 16″ between centers, made straight, and all to be well nailed. All necessary grounds are to be put on to fully prepare for plastering. All other places requiring it are to be furred in a proper manner.

LATHING AND PLASTERING.

All the walls and ceilings throughout the house are to be lathed with good pine or spruce laths, assorted so as to be entirely free from knots, in all of the principal rooms. All are to be plastered with a heavy coat of lime and hair mortar evenly floated, and skim-coated with beach sand finish. All angles are to be made straight and true.

There are to be stucco cornices and centerpieces in the front hall, parlor, and sitting-room. The cornices to cost, on an average, 37 cents per foot, and the centerpieces to cost, in the aggregate, $25.

INSIDE FINISH.

The inside finish is to be of clear and thoroughly kiln-dried pine lumber. The style of finish is to be as shown on detail drawings and put up in a thorough and workmanlike manner. There is to be a moulded base in all of the principal rooms throughout the house. All of the clothes closets are to have shelves and drawers as marked on the plans, and to have two strips on all sides where there are no drawers or shelves and provided with hooks screwed on not over 8″ apart. The store room and china closet are to be finished with drawers and shelves. The sink is to be finished with a closet underneath. The under floors are to be of good, sound, seasoned square-edged pine or spruce mill-planed boards, laid edge to edge. The upper floors are to be of narrow widths of seasoned pine, mill-planed, jointed, well laid and smoothed off. All floors are to be cut in between the bases.

The bath-tub, water-closet and wash-stand in the bath-room are to be finished with black walnut. The water-closet seat and the tub are to be paneled and moulded. The wash-bowl case is to be finished with drawers and a closet underneath. There is to be a paper box in the water-closet seat.

The front outside doors are to be double and of the sizes marked on the plan, to be 1¾" thick and to have raised mouldings. The upper panels are to be of glass. The rear outside door is to be of such size as marked on the plan 1¾" thick and moulded with raised mouldings. All other doors throughout the house are to be 1½" thick and moulded with raised mouldings. All doors are to be of such sizes as are figured on the plans and to have glass panels where marked.

All doors are to be of the best quality of kiln-dried pine lumber.

STAIRS.

The stairs are to be located and built as shown on the plans. They are to be finished with good clear pine lumber and to have a 7" (shaft measurement) chamfered newel post, 4" moulded rail and 1¾" fancy turned balusters, all to be of thoroughly seasoned black walnut. The landing and gallery posts are to be 5" and chamfered.

The cellar stairs are to be built in a good and substantial manner.

Build and set up the steps to front and back doors with good, sound, seasoned 2" hard pine plank. The front steps to have a moulding under the treads with returned nosings.

HARDWARE.

All doors are to be hung with good loose-jointed butts of suitable sizes for their respective places, and to have brass bolt mortise locks with brass plate and keys, and all to have pressed glass knobs and bronzed trimmings. The front doors to be trimmed with flush bolts and to have a lock with night-latch and furnished with duplicate keys. The knobs on the outside to be silvered glass with silver-plated trimmings. The knob inside is to be of pressed glass.

The front door is to be provided with a bell hung in such place as may be directed. The pull is to be of silvered glass and to correspond with the front door knobs.

GAS PIPES.

Gas pipes are to be put into the ceiling of the parlor, sitting room, front hall and kitchen, and in all other rooms where marked on the plans.

PLUMBING.

There is to be a 2′ × 4′ cast-iron sink at the end of the pantry to be furnished with a 1½" waste-pipe, cesspool strainer, etc., to make the same complete.

There is to be a 3" copper pump at the sink to be provided with a 1½′ bore, 2½ lb. lead pipe to connect with the well.

There is to be a 2½" force pump of the best quality, provided with a two ways faucet and 1½" galvanized iron suction pipe connecting with the rain water cistern.

The rising main connecting with the cistern in the bath-room is to be 1¼" in diameter, 2½ lbs. per foot.

The bath-room is to be fitted up with bath-tub, water-closet and wash-bowl. The bath-tub is to be of the usual size, lined with planished copper and furnished with a ⅝" brass faucet, plug, chain, and rose overflow.

The water-closet is to be the best pan closet with wedgwood basin, strong lead trap and 4" iron soil pipe and is to be provided with all necessary pipes, service boxes, and other fixtures to make the same complete in every respect.

The wash-bowl is to be 15" of marbled pattern, to have a countersunk marble top 1" thick with moulded edge and to have 8" marble back and ends. The faucet, chain, holder and plug are to be silver-plated. The wash-bowl case is to be lined up underneath with lead 4″ high and to have a suitable sized waste pipe connecting with the soil pipe.

There is to be a cistern over the bath-room of 300 gallons capacity, lined with 5 lb. sheet lead and to be provided with all the necessary pipes, valves, etc., to make the same complete in every respect.

The supply pipe for the bath-tub is to be ¾″ bore, 2½ lbs. per foot, for wash-bowl ⅜″ bore, 1½ lbs. per foot. The waste pipes for tub and bowl are to be 1½″ bore 3 lbs. per foot. All materials of good quality necessary to complete the plumber's work in every respect are to furnished and all the work is to be done in a good and workmanlike manner.

PAINTING AND GLAZING.

All of the woodwork outside and inside that is usually painted, is to have three good coats of paint of the best quality all to be tinted as may be directed. The closet floors are to be painted. All gutters and tinned roofs are to be painted with three good coats of paint. The blinds are to be painted four coats of such color as may be directed. The stair rails and all hard woodwork are to be filled and well rubbed down in oil. All hard pine work is to be puttied and well oiled.

All of the sashes are to be glazed with the best German glass, all to be well bedded, bradded and back puttied. The front doors are to be glazed with ground glass of such pattern as may be selected. All other glass panel doors are to have plain ground glass.

FINALLY.

It is to be understood that everything necessary to the full and complete execution of the work according to the general intent and meaning of these plans and specifications is to be done and all materials furnished so as to complete the work in a good and workmanlike manner whether herein particularly described or not.

FORM OF CONTRACT

Memorandum of agreement made between A. B., of ———, in the County of ———, and Commonwealth of ———, of the first part, and C. D., of ———, in the county and commonwealth aforesaid, builder, of the second part, touching the erection of a wooden dwelling house for said A. B., to be located on ——— street, in ———, and to completely finish the same in all its parts by the party of the second part, according to the full intent and meaning of the plans and specifications of even date herewith and signed by both parties hereto, said plans and specifications to be considered as a part of this agreement.

The said C. D., in consideration of the covenants and agreements hereinafter contained by the said A. B. to be kept and performed, does covenant, promise and agree that he the said C. D. shall commence the work immediately and prosecute it to its completion without any delays of the same, except such as are inevitably caused by the strike of workmen or the state of the weather, and that he will perform all labor and furnish all materials necessary to complete the work so as to satisfy the provisions of this contract in accordance with the requirements of the plans and specifications in the most thorough and workmanlike manner under the superintendence of

to his satisfaction and to the acceptance of the owner on or before the ——— day of ——— now next ensuing the date hereof. And it is hereby expressly agreed that the said C. D. shall pay and allow the said A. B. for each and every day (except the aforesaid) beyond said ——— of ——— the sum of ten dollars as liquidate damages. But if the work is delayed by causes aforesaid, the said C. D. is to be allowed one extra day for each and every day of delay to complete said work.

And the said A. B. in consideration of the above premises doth for himself and his executors agree well and truly to pay or cause to be paid unto the said C. D. or his legal representatives the following sum to wit: Three thousand eight hundred dollars in the manner following, that is to say, when the cellar is finished and the building raised and boarded, one thousand dollars: when the outside is completed one thousand dollars: when the plastering is finished eight hundred dollars, and the balance one thousand dollars in thirty days after the building is completed and accepted by the architect and proprietor free from all charges by way of lien or other attachments.

No extra work shall be performed or materials furnished beyond that provided for by this agreement and the plans and specifications aforesaid, nor shall the work be changed or in anywise varied by the said C. D., except upon request made by the said A. B., who shall have the right to vary and alter so far as respects any part of the work or materials at any time remaining to be performed or finished by the said C. D. And in case a request is made by said A. B. to have any change or alterations made, the price shall be agreed upon and the bargain made in writing and signed by both parties hereto before such changes or alterations are commenced. And if any difference of opinion shall arise in regard to the price of extra work, it shall be referred to the architect and two disinterested persons, one to be chosen by each of the parties hereto and whose decision shall be final and binding upon all parties.

It is further agreed that insurance shall be effected upon the building in some company approved by the said A. B., immediately after the first payments to the amount of that payment, and to be increased after each payment to the amount of the sum of all the payments then made. Said policy of insurance is to be in the name and for the benefit of said A. B. in case of loss, he paying one half and the said C. D. paying one half the expense of the policy.

In witness whereof the said parties of the first and second parts have hereunto set their hands and seals this ——— day of ——— one thousand eight hundred and

Executed in presence of

PLATES 3, 4.

DESIGN FOR A COTTAGE.

BROWN & GRABLE, Architects, 307 Locust Street, St. Louis.

Plate 3. Shows the front elevation and first story plan, containing Hall, Parlor, Library, Dining-room, Conservatory, Kitchen, Pantry, &c.

Plate 4. Side elevation and second story plan, containing four Chambers, Bath-room and Closets.

Scale—eight feet to the inch.   Cost, built of brick, $6,000.

Plate 3.

FRONT ELEVATION

KITCHEN
12' x 16"

CONSERVATORY
11' x 11'

PANTRY
7'6" x 8'6"

HALL
8' x 8'

PORCH

DINING ROOM
16' x 18'

HALL
10'

PARLOR
16' x 18'

HALL
6'

PORCH

LIBRARY
16' x 16'

PORCH

I^st STORY PLAN

Plate 4.

SIDE ELEVATION.

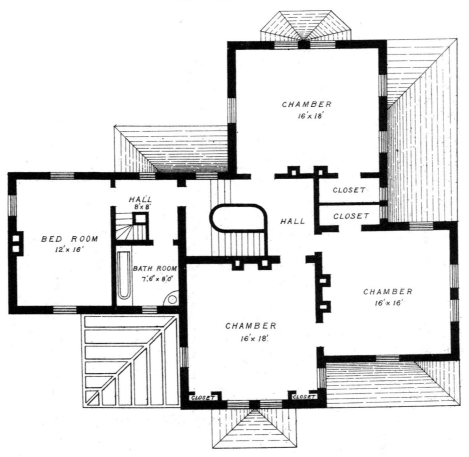

CHAMBER
16' x 18'

CLOSET

CLOSET

HALL
8' x 8'

HALL

BED ROOM
12' x 16'

BATH ROOM
7'6" x 8'0"

CHAMBER
16' x 16'

CHAMBER
16' x 18'

CLOSET   CLOSET

2ᴰ STORY PLAN.

Lith by J Bien 16 & 18 Park Place N.Y.

SPECIFICATIONS.

SPECIFICATIONS of the Materials to be Furnished and Labor to be Performed in the Erection and Completion of a one and a half story Cottage, in the Gothic style, for Mr. ——, in the City of St. Louis, State of Missouri. (See Plates Three and Four for the elevations and plans.)

GENERAL DESCRIPTION.

The building will have a frontage on Lafayette Avenue of forty-three feet, by a depth of fifty feet, there will be a cellar under the entire building 7' 6" deep, the first story will be 11' high, the second story will be 10' high to underside of cellar beams; all these heights to be in the clear when finished. For position of doors and windows and arrangement of rooms reference is hereby had to plans.

EXCAVATION.

The earth to be dug out the proper depth and extent to receive the cellar and foundation walls, dig trenches for footing courses under all walls two feet wide and six inches deep; all earth not required to fill in around walls and to grade lot to be carted away. The cellar to be dug 5' below the grade of lot, cesspool to be 7' diameter and 15' deep.

RUBBLE STONE WORK.

All the cellar and foundation walls are to be built up straight and plumb to the under side of sill eighteen inches thick, the footings six inches deep and two feet wide; the work to be of the best quality of quarry building limestone, laid up with fresh lime and sharp sand mortar, and all joints well pointed, and the work well bonded with through stone, the top course to be of broad flat rock not less than three feet thick, the outside of walls where exposed to be tuck pointed.

TIMBER WORK.

All timber used throughout to be of a sound quality and as well seasoned as can be procured, and of the following dimensions:—The sills to be 4" × 6"; the first and second tier of joist to be 2" × 10", properly framed and placed 16" from centers; the second tier of joist will be notched on a 1" × 6" ribbon piece let in the side studding; the collar beams will be 2" × 6" spiked to side of rafters; the wall plate will be 2" × 4" spiked to top of studding; the studding will be 2" × 6" placed 16" from centers; the corner posts will be 4" × 6" framed in sill; the braces 3" × 4" framed in corner posts and sill, draw bored and pinned; the rafters 2" × 6" properly framed and well secured to wall plate, and placed 16" from centers, secured at the top to 2" × 8" ridge piece. Each tier of joist will have one row of cross bridging through the center of 1½" × 2", well nailed to joist, the perch timbers will be 2" × 6" properly framed and put up as shown.

SIDING.

The building enclosed with second rate dressed white pine weather boarding and to have 1¼" lap at joints.

ROOFING.

The roof will be sheathed with 1" sheathing boards, and covered with the best quality of white pine sawed shingles laid 4½" to the weather with the joints well broken.

FLOORING.

The floors will be laid with the best second-rate white pine mill-worked flooring, well seasoned and laid in courses of not over 5½" wide, well nailed to each joist and cleaned off, when finished; the perch floors will be laid in courses of not over 3½" wide, with white lead in the joints.

CORNICES.

Prepare and put eave gable and porch cornices as shown, of good well-seasoned white pine free from sap or large knots ; prepare gutter beds for metal gutters, as shown.

PLASTERING.

All the rooms to be lathed with pine laths, and to have two coats of brown mortar, and skim with plaster paris—finish well with trowel ; all angles to be made straight and plumb.

WINDOWS.

All the windows throughout to have double hung box frames, the sash 1¾'' thick and made as shown, the sizes as shown on elevation, and hung with 1¾ axle pulleys and patent sash cord ; each window to have sash locks to cost $ per dozen. All the windows throughout will be provided with outside rolling slat blinds, 1⅜'' thick, hung with patent spiral blind hinges, and well fastened. The cellar windows will have solid 2'' plank frames, with 1⅜'' sash made in two parts, and hung with loose butts and fastened with good bolts ; the exterior finish of frames will be as shown.

BAY WINDOWS.

To be constructed as shown on plan ; the roofs will be covered with the best roofing tin, painted on the under sides.

PORCHES.

Put up as shown on drawings, of good sound white pine lumber, well seasoned ; the under side of roof ceiled with matched boards, smoothed and beaded ; the roofs will be covered the same as bay windows. The steps will be made of 1¼'' white pine.

CONSERVATORY.

Built as shown on plan and elevation ; the sashes of sides made 1¾'' thick, and hung on pivots in center of sides ; the roof will be of glass, properly set in sky-light sash, and arranged for proper ventilation.

TIN WORK.

Put in eave gutters of one cross leaded tin 14'' wide, well painted on both sides ; put up down spouts, 3½'' diameter, at the several points where required, with proper elbows.

INTERIOR FINISH.

The inside finish will be of good second-rate white pine, well seasoned ; the rooms and hall of main building, first story, will be finished with a neat moulded casing 8'' wide, and 11'' moulded base ; the second story will have plain 6'' moulded casing, 7'' moulded base ; the kitchen, servants' and bath-rooms finished with a plain 5'' casing, and 6'' beaded base ; the windows of main house will have moulded panel backs, the others finished to stool and apron pieces.

DOORS.

All doors throughout will be made in four panels and moulded on both sides. Those on first story will be 3' × 7' 6'', 1¾'' thick ; those in the second story, 2' 10'' × 6' 10'' ; the closet doors will be as large as the spaces will properly admit ; the front door will be made the same style as shown, there will be raised mouldings on the outside. All doors to be hung to 2'' rabbeted frames, with proper butts, and to have hard wood carpet strips. The locks in the first story will be 5'' mortise, with white and silver-plated trimming ; all others will have 5'' tumbler rim locks, with brown knobs and bronze trimming ; the outside doors to be secured with suitable bolts.

PAINTING.

All wood and other work usually painted to have three good coats of lead and oil paint of any color the owner may desire. All interior finish of doors and windows, with the door, frames inside of sash and base, will be grained in oak, neat style and varnished ; the blinds painted Paris green.

GLAZING.

All windows to be glazed with the best quality of Pittsburgh glass, well tinned, bedded, and back puttied.

MANTLES.

The three principal rooms of the first story will be provided with marble mantles, to cost $75 each; those in the second story to have a neat wooden mantle, to cost $12 each.

GRATES.

The grates of first story to cost $14 each, those in second story $12 each—to be three in each story—these prices to be exclusive of the setting; they are to be set with fire brick in the best manner.

CHIMNEYS.

Are to be built of good brick, as shown; the flues to be 9″ × 12″, well pargeted on the inside work in a 6″ thimble in kitchen flue; the chimneys topped out with best quality of red brick and surmounted with chimney tops of terra cotta.

GAS PIPES.

To be run through the building so as to furnish light for each room and halls, the outlets will be placed where the owner may desire, the pipes to be the sizes required by gas companies' regulations.

BELLS.

There will be two bells in the building—one to front door, and one in parlor.

STAIRS.

The stairs will be built on strong carriages. The main stairs will be of clear yellow pine, 1″ thick for the treads, and $\frac{7}{8}$″ white pine risers, finished with return nosing scotia and fillets; the rail will be $2\frac{1}{8}$″ thick, $4\frac{1}{4}$″ wide moulded; the balusters will be $1\frac{3}{4}$″ fancy turned base and neck; the newell will be 10″, with turned base and cap, and octagon panel shaft; and all to be of well seasoned black walnut. The steps and risers will be housed in the wall-string, the stairs will be enclosed underneath with a panelled and moulded spandrill; the rear steps will be of yellow pine and white pine risers, finished with plain turned balusters and 2″ × 3″ walnut hand rail; 7″ turned newell post, of black walnut. Those stairs will be enclosed underneath with matched ceiling boards, smoothed and beaded, with a door leading to cellar by a strong stairway with plain rail.

PLUMBERS' WORK.

There will be a 6′ copper planished bath-tub, fitted up in bath-room, with all the necessary supply, and waste-pipe and compression draw-cocks for hot and cold water; also fitted up in kitchen, a 40 gallon copper boiler, with all necessary pipe to connect to bath-tub, sink and wash-basin; also put up in bath-room, a marble top wash-basin with supply and waste-pipe, and draw-cocks of an approved kind; and also fit up an iron sink in the kitchen, with supply-pipe for hot and cold water, and $1\frac{1}{2}$″ waste-pipe. All supply-pipe will be extra strong $\frac{5}{8}$″; the waste water from bath-room and kitchen will be conducted to sewer running through the cellar; the sewer will be of 12″ stone drain-pipe, and will be continued from the cellar to cesspool in yard.

CLOSETS.

The closets will be fitted up with shelves, strips, and clothes hooks as desired; the store-rooms and china closet will be shelved as may be required; close up under sink and hang small door and fasten with spring catch.

CONDITIONS.

That all material and labor used are to be the best of their respective kinds, and if there is anything omitted in these specifications, or that is not fully shown on the plans, which should be necessary for the full completion of the building, according to the full intent and meaning of these specifications and accompanying drawings, the same is to be done at the expense of the contractor without extra charge; and, in case of any alteration, addition, or deduction, the price shall be agreed upon in writing before going into effect; and no extras will be allowed unless first agreed upon, and the price fixed. The work to be under the superintendence of Alfred Grable, architect, who will have power to reject any material or labor which, in his opinion, is not in accordance with these specifications.

APPROVED FORM OF CONTRACT

ADOPTED BY THE ST. LOUIS CO-OPERATIVE BUILDING ASSOCIATION.

ARTICLES OF AGREEMENT, made and entered into this   day of   Eighteen hundred and sixty eight, by and between the SAMUEL P. SIMPSON party of the First part, and Messrs. BROWN AND GRABLE with D. T. WRIGHT, as security party of the Second part, all of the city and county of St. Louis, State of Missouri, in the words and figures as follows:

The said party of the Second part, covenant and agree to and with the said party of the First part, to make and erect, build and finish a certain two story brick dwelling house on a certain lot of ground, situated on McPherson Avenue, between Warne and Sarah Avenues, for SAMUEL P. SIMPSON, Esq., in accordance with the drawings, plans and elevations, and specifications furnished by the superintending architect, and adopted for said buildings, which are hereto annexed and made a part of this contract.

The said party of the Second part, shall at their own cost and charges, provide and deliver all and every kind of material of good and sound quality and description, together with the cartage, scaffolding, tackles, tools, templets, rules, moulds, matters and things, labor and work, which may be necessary for the due, proper and complete execution of this contract, and accordingly erect, build, finish and complete in a good, sound, workmanlike manner to the perfect satisfaction and approbation of the superintendent, J. H. McCLAREN Esq., the aforesaid buildings and works, according to the specifications, drawings, dimensions and explanations and observations thereon, or herein stated, described or implied or incident thereto, which may become necessary to the true intent and meaning thereof, although not specially and specifically stated or described by the aforesaid drawings and specifications.

And should it appear, that any of the works hereby intended to be done, or matters relative thereto are not fully detailed or explained in the said specifications and drawings, the said party of the Second part shall apply to the superintendent for such further detailed explanations, and perform his orders as part of this contract.

The superintendent shall be at liberty to make any deviation from or alteration in the plan, form, construction, detail and execution, described by the drawings and specifications, without invaliding or rendering void this contract, and in case of any difference in the expense, an addition to or abatement from the contract price shall be made, and the same shall be determined by the architect.

And the said superintendent shall have full power and lawful authority to reject the whole or any part or portion of said materials or work, which may not in his opinion be in strict accordance with the letter and spirit of these presents; and if by reason of any act or deed on the part of the said party of the Second part, the said party of the First part, or its legal representatives, or the superintendent, shall be led to believe that the erection or completion of said buildings is retarded unnecessarily, they or either of them may, as often as the same appears to them necessary, furnish such works and materials as they may deem necessary to facilitate the completion of said buildings, and the cost and expense thereof is to be borne by and chargeable to the party of the Second part exclusively.

And in case of any alteration or change that may be directed by the said superintendent as aforesaid in the plans, drawings and construction of the aforesaid buildings, and in case of any omission or addition to said buildings being required by said superintendent, the cost and expense thereof is to be agreed upon in writing, and such agreement is to be signed by said party of the Second part and superintendent before the same is done, or before any allowance therefor can be claimed; and in case of any failure so to agree, the same shall be completed upon the original plan

And in case of frost or inclemency of weather, the said party of the Second part shall effectually cover, protect and secure the several works, as occasion may require, and prevent admission of wet through the apertures, and all damages occasioned thereby or otherwise, during the progress of the works and by depredation or fire, the same to be borne and reinstated by and at the expense of the said party of the Second part who shall also case effectually with boarding all bases, capitals, cornices and other projections, and deliver up the building in the most perfect order and condition, fit for use and occupation.

The said St. Louis Co-operative Building Association reserves to itself the right to insure said buildings, during the progress of the works at the costs and expenses of the said party of the Second part.

The work of erecting and finishing said buildings, including all alterations and additions in said contract provided or hereafter agreed upon, is to be proceeded with, with all reasonable dispatch, and the same shall be completed and delivered up to said party of the first part in perfect order and condition, fit for use and occupation on or before the first day of May, of the year Eighteen hundred and sixty-nine, it being agreed that the said party of the Second part shall forfeit the sum of ten dollars for every day expiring after that day, before the completion and delivery of said buildings as aforesaid to the said party of the First part, and this condition not to be made or rendered void by any alteration or additional works being performed, but in such case the time shall be extended as shall be deemed proper by the superintendent and agreed to by the said party of the Second part, at the time of such extension.

The superintendent's opinion, certificate report, and decision on all matters to be binding and conclusive on the party of the Second part.

The said party of the First part agrees and binds itself for and in consideration of the erection of said buildings as aforesaid to pay unto the party of the Second part the sum of seven thousand two hundred and sixty dollars ($7,260).

Payments to be made as the work progresses to the amount of the value of sixty per cent. of the work done, as the superintendent shall estimate it, and 20 per cent. of the contract amount at the completion and delivery of the work, and the residue of 20 per cent., or the balance of the contract price six months after the buildings are completed, and delivered up to the said party of the First part, but the said party of the first part shall have the right at any time after said buildings are completed to settle with and pay said party of the Second part, either in cash or by notes, as may be agreed upon by both parties. It being, however, understood that nothing herein contained shall be in any way so construed as to require the deferred payment to be made in less than six months after the completion and acceptance of the buildings by the party of the First part.

The portion of the contract price contemplated to be paid during the progress of the work, to be paid in instalments and dates as follows, provided that at such dates the progress of the work has made such payments due :—Eight hundred ($800) dollars when the first floor joist is on, eight hundred ($800) dollars when the second floor joist is on, eight hundred ($800) dollars when the roof is on, eight hundred and sixty ($860) dollars when the building is plastered, one thousand ($1,000) dollars when the finish and trimmings are up, fifteen hundred ($1,500) dollars when the building is completed, and the balance as hereinbefore provided for.

Provided, that the wages of artisans and laborers, and all those employed by, or furnishing materials to the said party of the Second part, shall have been paid and satisfied, so that they shall have no lien upon the buildings or works, and in case the said party of the Second part shall fail so to pay and satisfy all and every claim and demand against said buildings as aforesaid, the said party of the First part may, if it deems proper so to do, retain from the moneys due and coming to said party of the Second part, enough to pay and satisfy such claims and demands, it being, however, understood that nothing herein contained shall in any way be construed as impairing the right of the said party of the First part to hold the said party of the Second part, or securities liable on their bond for any breach of the conditions of the same.

Sub-contractors and parties furnishing materials on account of this contract are to be paid by the party of the First part, pro rata, as above stated, upon order from the party of the Second part, and all such payments to be charged to account of this contract.

All payments by the party of the First part to the party of the Second part, or to their orders to be made upon orders from the said superintendent.

In Witness Whereof, we, the several parties to tne above contract, have set our hands and seals, the day and year first above written.

WITNESS.

JAMES H. McCLAREN.

BROWN & GRABLE.   [Seal]

D. T. WRIGHT.   [Seal]

P. S.—The above is a copy of contract for the building of a house for Gen'l. Samuel P. Simpson, designed by Alfred Grable, Architect, 416 Locust St., St. Louis, Mo.

PLATE 5.

DESIGN FOR ITALIAN COTTAGE.

E. R. FRANCISCO, Architect, Kansas City, Mo.

Plate 5. Shows the front and side elevations and plans.

Scale of elevations—one-eighth inch to the foot.

Scale of plans---three-thirty-second of an inch to the foot.   Cost, built of wood, $2,000.   Brick, $2,500.

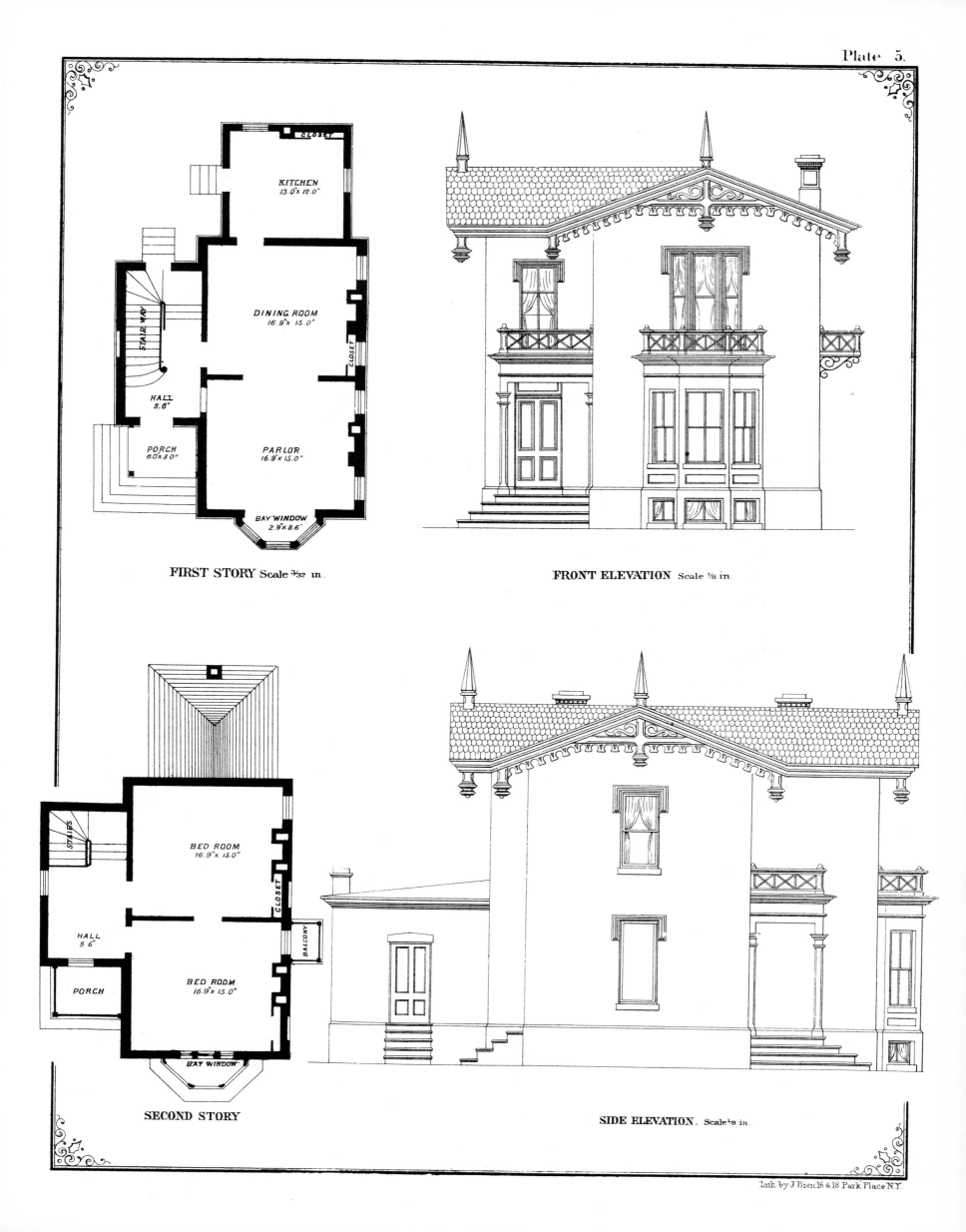

Plate 5.

FIRST STORY Scale 3/32 in.

FRONT ELEVATION Scale 1/8 in.

SECOND STORY

SIDE ELEVATION. Scale 1/8 in.

CLOSET

KITCHEN
13.0" x 12.0"

STAIR WAY

DINING ROOM
16.9" x 15.0"

CLOSET

HALL
8.6"

PORCH
6.0" x 8.0"

PARLOR
16.9" x 15.0"

BAY WINDOW
2.9" x 8.6"

STAIRS

BED ROOM
16.9" x 15.0"

CLOSET

BALCONY

HALL
8.6"

PORCH

BED ROOM
16.9" x 15.0"

BAY WINDOW

Lith. by J. Bien 16 & 18 Park Place N.Y.

PLATE 6.

C. Edward Loth, Architect, Troy, N.Y.

Fig. 1. Front elevation of one-story frame cottage.   Cost, $1,600.

Fig. 2. Side elevation.

Fig. 3. First floor plan.

Fig. 4. Front elevation of two-story frame house.   Cost, $2,250.

Fig. 5. First floor plan.

Fig. 6. Second floor plan.

The designs on this plate are drawn to scale of three-thirty-second of an inch to the foot.

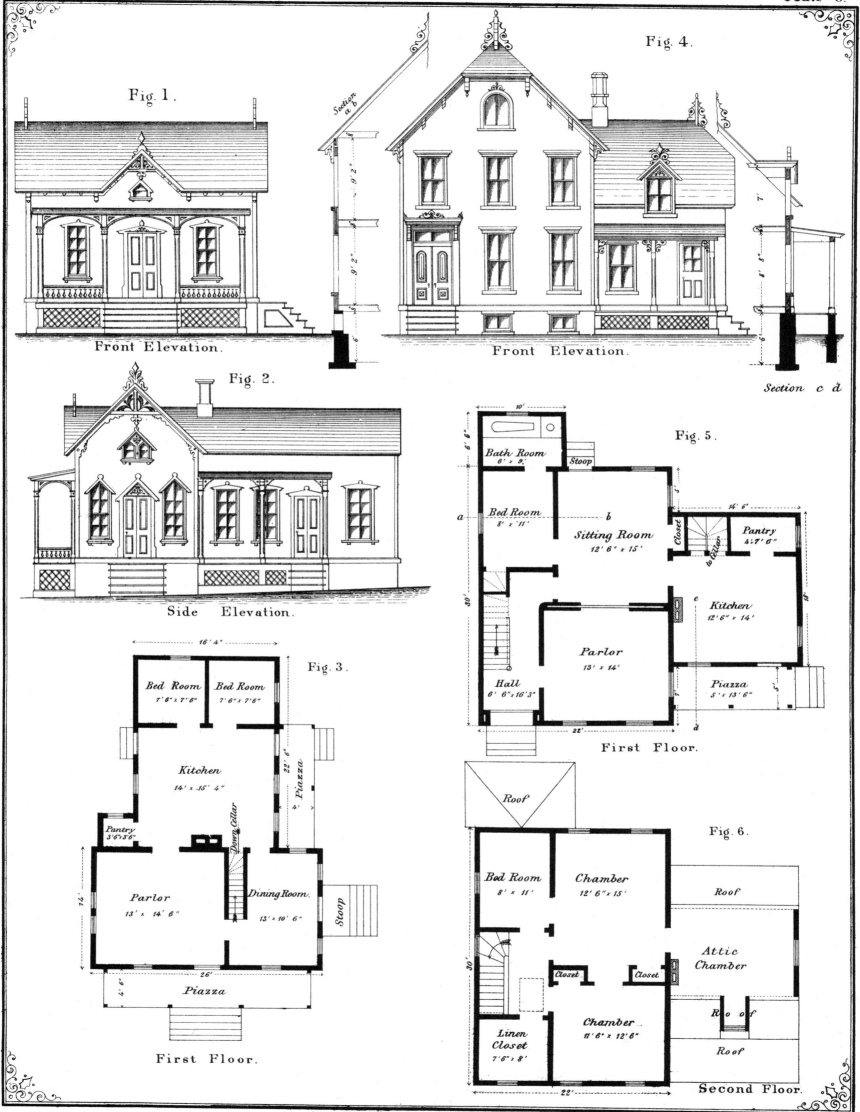

Plate 6.

Fig. 1.

Front Elevation.

Fig. 4.

Section a b

Front Elevation.

Section c d

Fig. 2.

Side Elevation.

Fig. 5.

Bath Room
6' x 9'

Stoop

Bed Room
8' x 11'

Sitting Room
12' 6" x 15'

Closet

to Cellar

Pantry
4' x 7' 6"

Kitchen
12' 6" x 14'

Parlor
13' x 14'

Hall
6' 6" x 16' 3"

Piazza
5' x 13' 6"

First Floor.

Fig. 3.

Bed Room
7' 6" x 7' 6"

Bed Room
7' 6" x 7' 6"

Kitchen
14' x 15' 4"

Piazza

Down Cellar

Pantry
3' 6" x 5' 6"

Parlor
13' x 14' 6"

Dining Room
13' x 10' 6"

Stoop

Piazza

First Floor.

Fig. 6.

Roof

Bed Room
8' x 11'

Chamber
12' 6" x 15'

Roof

Closet

Closet

Attic Chamber

Linen Closet
7' 6" x 8'

Chamber
11' 6" x 12' 6"

Roof

Roof

Second Floor.

Lith by J. Bien 16 & 18 Park Place N.Y.

PLATES 7, 8, 9.

ELEVATIONS, PLANS AND DETAILS FOR A GOTHIC COTTAGE.

EDGAR BERRYMAN, Architect, 388 Main Street, Buffalo.

Plate 7. Fig. 1 is the front elevation; Fig. 2 A, Vestibule; B, Hall eight feet wide containing main stairs and recess (a) for hat rack; C, Parlor fifteen by eighteen feet; D, Dining-room sixteen by nineteen feet; E, Bed or Sitting-room having large closet H, and Bath-room G, in connection; F, Kitchen; I, Closet; K, Pantry; L, Serving and China Closet; W, rear platform; N, Verandah; height main part eleven feet, rear nine feet four inches.

Plate 8. Fig. 3 side elevation; Fig. 4 V, Platform on level of second floor of rear part; U and T, Bed-rooms; X, Closets; Q, R, S, Chambers; P, Tower containing stairs to Observatory; O, Hall containing niche for Statuary. All on Plates 7 and 8 are drawn twelve feet to an inch.

Plate 9. Contains principal details; A, Tower and gable windows; B, Railing and cornice of Observatory; C, Elevation and section of cornice and butments on Bay windows; D, Main cornice; E, Finial; F, Verandah; G, Chimney tops; L, Stair-case. All one-half inch to the foot. H, O, N, Section of Doors; M and I, Inside finish; K, section of window frame; P, Bases; S, Window-sill; I, Water-table all one and one-half inch to the foot; Q, Plaster cornice and panel moulding; R, Plaster arch over Bay windows and in Hall.

Plate 7.

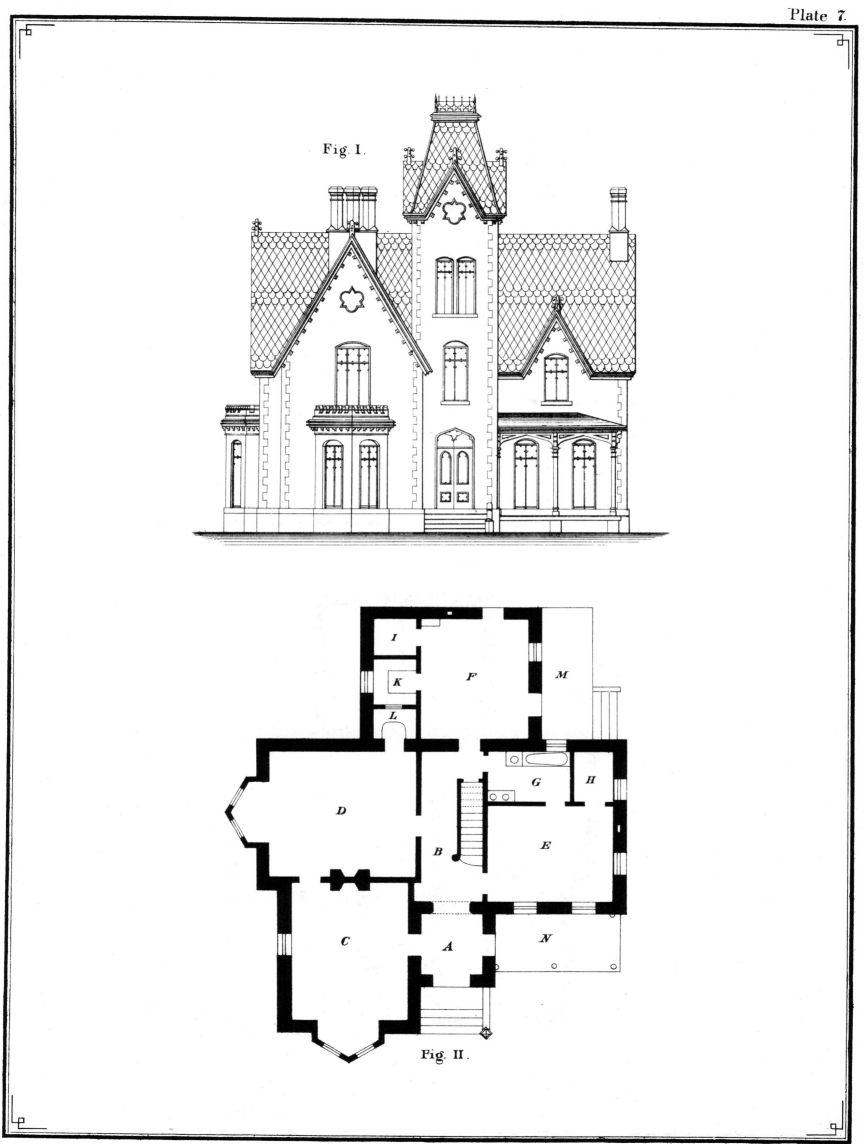

Fig. I.

Fig. II.

Plate 8.

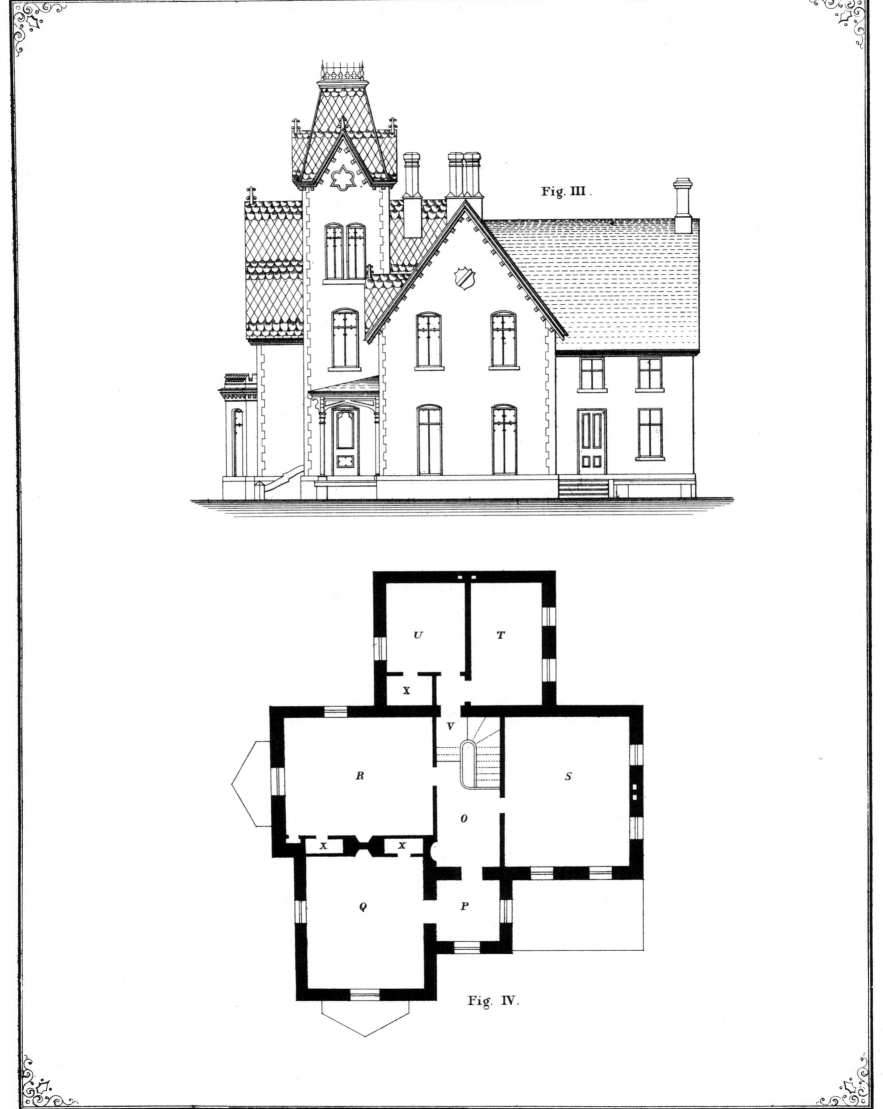

Fig. III.

Fig. IV.

Plate 9.

PLATES 10, 11, 12.

DESIGN FOR A FRAME COTTAGE VILLA.

A. C. BRUCE, Architect, Nashville, Tenn.

Plate 10. Shows the front elevation and first floor plan of a dwelling recently erected for Col. A. S. Colyer, President of the Sawannee Coal Mines. The arrangement has been made without regard to space. All the rooms are large and well ventilated. The doors to the Library and the one on the Parlor entering on the front porch are two folds with sash. The inside doors first story, are three by seven feet with transom over each and moulded on both sides. The front door is of black walnut; the sliding doors are also made of black walnut two and one-half inches thick, moulded below, with ornamental glass panels above. The windows are all double box hung with weights. The first story was plastered to ground when the finish, shown in detail C, was put on, out of first-class yellow pine oiled and varnished. The first story is twelve feet in clear. The plan on the plate is drawn to a scale of three thirty-second of one inch to the foot. The second story is finished with Poplar in a plain manner and neatly painted.

Plate 11. Side elevation and second story plan. Scale three thirty-second of one inch to the foot.

Plate 12. Details of Gable, Front Window, Vestibule and Finial at one-half of one inch to the foot. Section of Architrave at one and one-half inch. Cost $7,500.

Plate 10.

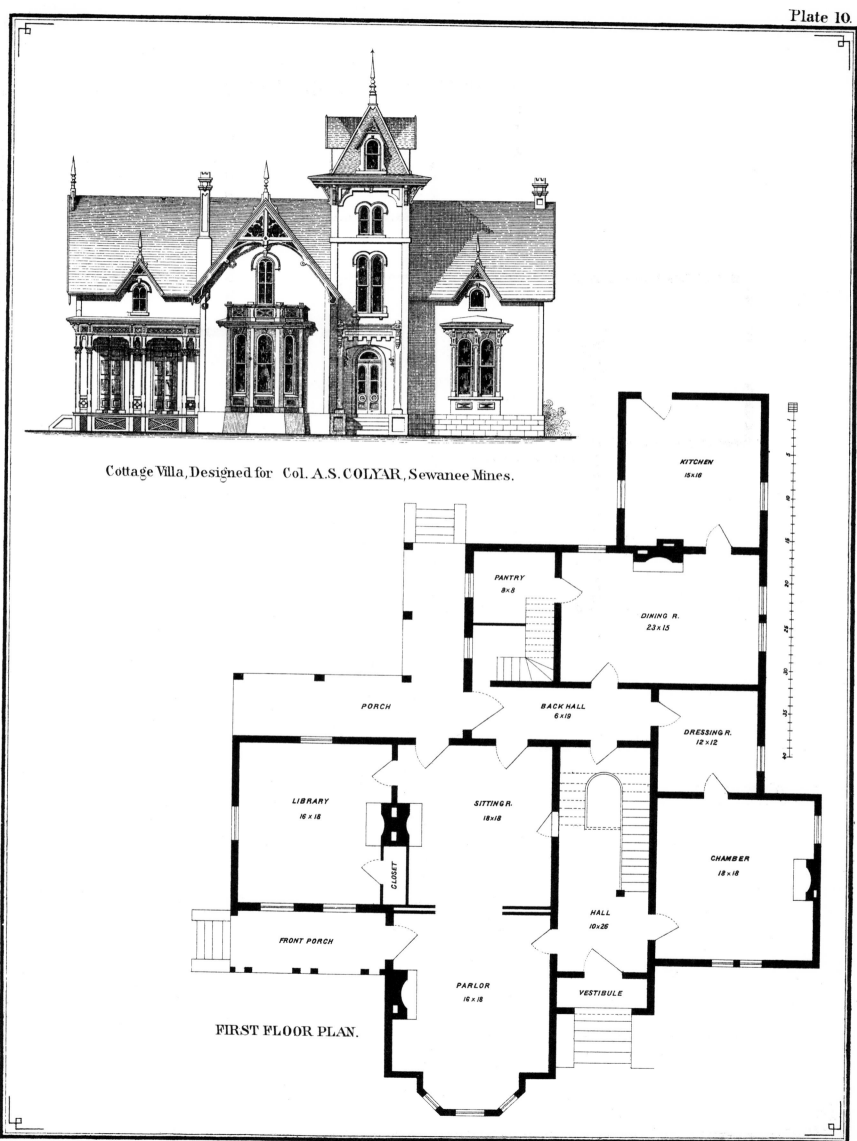

Cottage Villa, Designed for Col. A.S. COLYAR, Sewanee Mines.

KITCHEN
15x16

PANTRY
8x8

DINING R.
23x15

PORCH

BACK HALL
6x19

DRESSING R.
12x12

LIBRARY
16 x 18

SITTING R.
18x18

CLOSET

CHAMBER
18x18

FRONT PORCH

HALL
10x26

FIRST FLOOR PLAN.

PARLOR
16 x 18

VESTIBULE

J. Bien, Lith.

Plate 11.

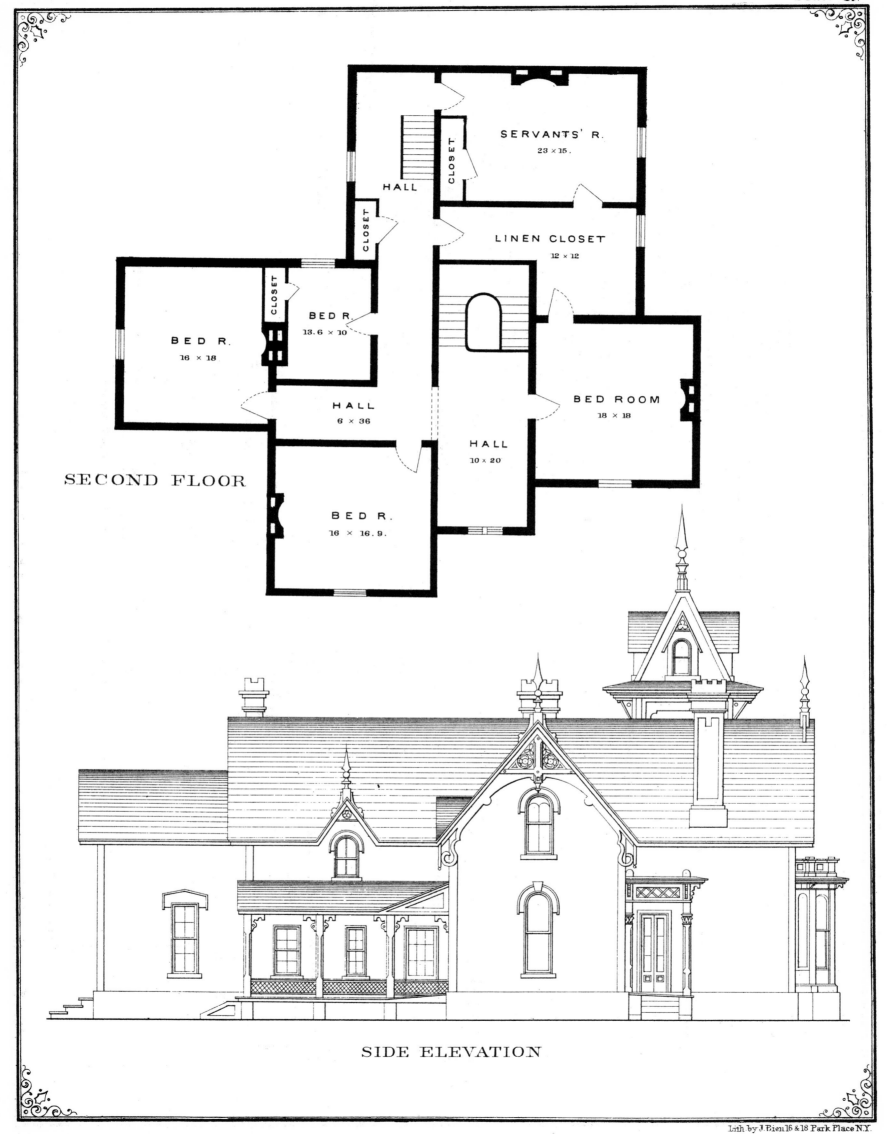

SERVANTS' R.
23 × 15.

HALL

CLOSET

CLOSET

LINEN CLOSET
12 × 12

CLOSET

BED R.
16 × 18

BED R.
13.6 × 10

BED ROOM
18 × 18

HALL
6 × 36

HALL
10 × 20

SECOND FLOOR

BED R.
16 × 16.9.

SIDE ELEVATION

Lith by J. Bien 16 & 18 Park Place N.Y.

Plate 12.

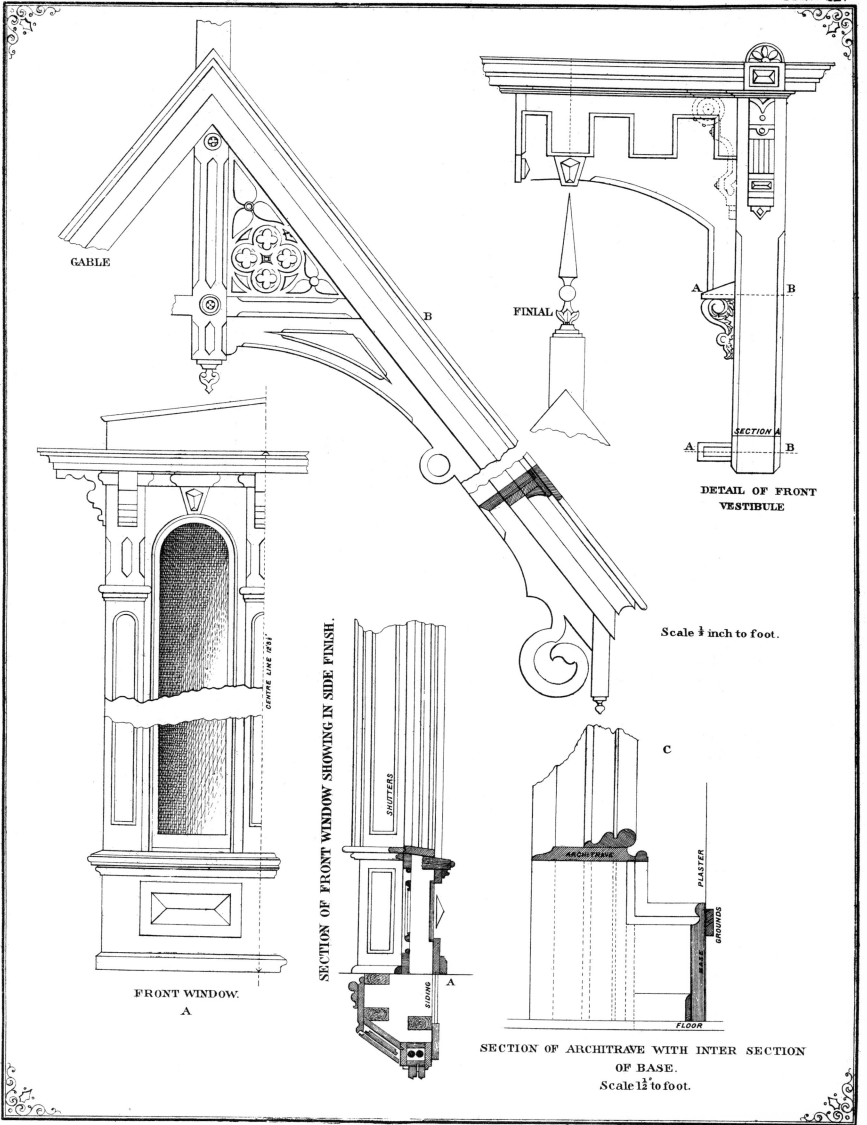

GABLE

FINIAL

DETAIL OF FRONT
VESTIBULE

Scale ⅓ inch to foot.

CENTRE LINE 128ᶦ

SECTION OF FRONT WINDOW SHOWING IN SIDE FINISH.

SHUTTERS

SIDING

A

FRONT WINDOW.

A

SECTION A

A   B

A   B

ARCHITRAVE

PLASTER

GROUNDS

BASE

FLOOR

C

SECTION OF ARCHITRAVE WITH INTER SECTION
OF BASE.
Scale 1½ to foot.

PLATES 13, 14.

DESIGN FOR A CHEAP RESIDENCE WITH FRENCH ROOF.

G. B. CROFF, Architect, Fort Edward, N. Y.

Plate 13. Contains the front elevation, first floor plan, and details of Cornice, Balustrade, Canopy, Window-caps, &c.

Plate 14. Shows the side elevation, plan of second floor and details for front and rear Verandah.

Scale of elevations and plans one-eighth of one inch to the foot. Details three-fourth of one inch to the foot.

This dwelling has recently been erected for John D. Bancroft, Cashier of the First National Bank of Ballston Spa, N. Y. Total cost including Architect's fees $4,000. The design presents a unique and inviting appearance and would voluntarily suggest an outlay of double the amount. The roof is covered with slate of the best quality. The frame is balloon constructed from two by four wallstrips and covered with good quality pine clap-boards, laying four inches to the weather. The first story is filled in with soft brick well laid in lime mortar. The floors are best quality Canada spruce. The exterior and interior details are of pine. The windows are hung with weights and supplied with finely finished inside blinds. The basement contains a hot-air furnace with four, nine by fourteen registers.

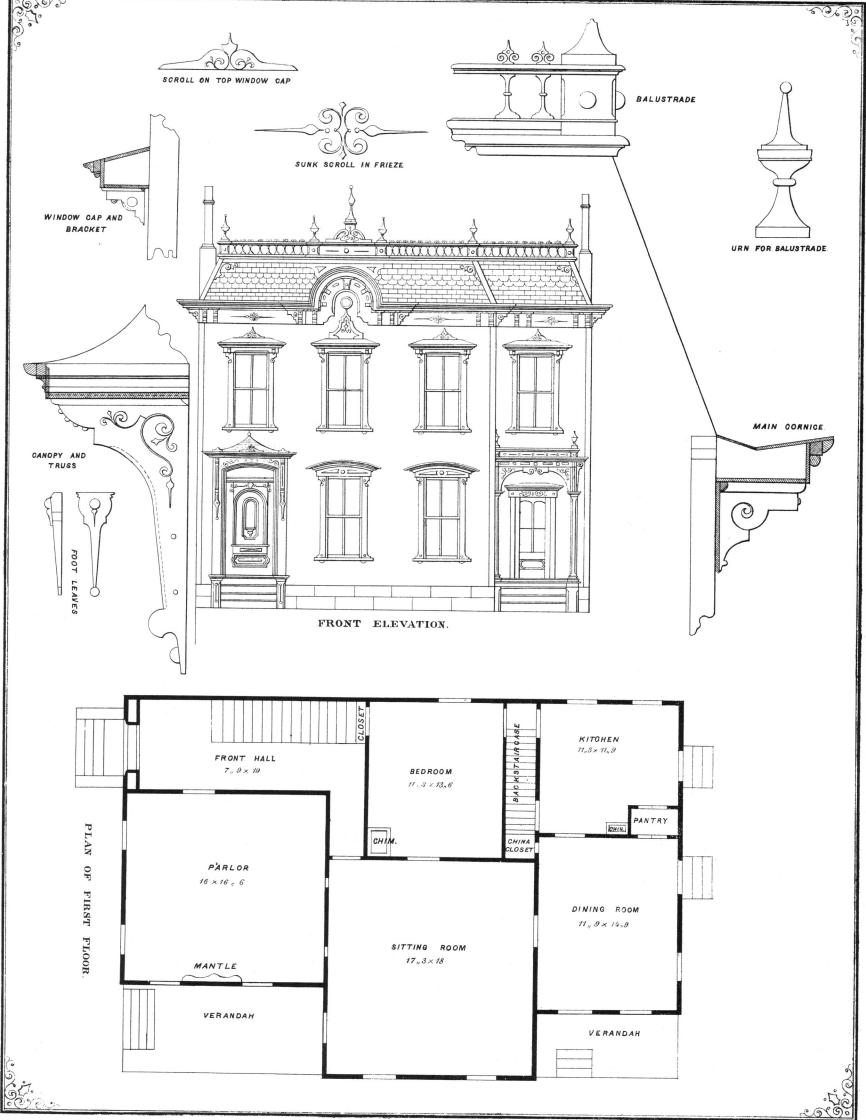

Plate 13

SCROLL ON TOP WINDOW CAP

SUNK SCROLL IN FRIEZE

BALUSTRADE

WINDOW CAP AND BRACKET

URN FOR BALUSTRADE.

CANOPY AND TRUSS

MAIN CORNICE.

FOOT LEAVES

FRONT ELEVATION.

PLAN OF FIRST FLOOR.

FRONT HALL
7,, 9 x 19

BEDROOM
11,, 3 x 13,, 6

KITCHEN
11,, 3 x 11,, 9

CLOSET

BACK STAIR CASE

CHIM.

PANTRY

CHIN.

CHINA CLOSET

PARLOR
16 x 16 ,, 6

SITTING ROOM
17,, 3 x 18

DINING ROOM
11,, 9 x 14,, 9

MANTLE

VERANDAH

VERANDAH

Lith. by J. Bien 16 & 18 Park Place N.Y.

Plate 14

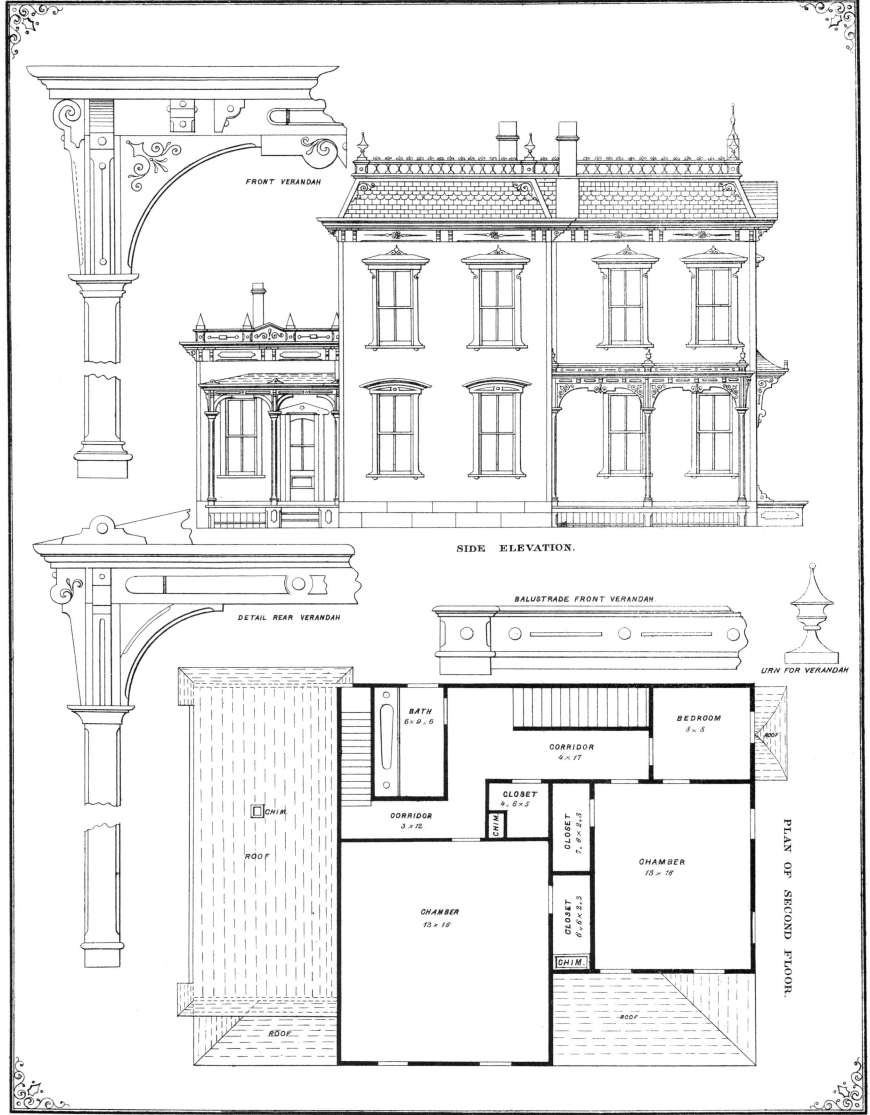

FRONT VERANDAH

SIDE ELEVATION.

DETAIL REAR VERANDAH

BALUSTRADE FRONT VERANDAH.

URN FOR VERANDAH

PLAN OF SECOND FLOOR.

BATH
6 × 9 „ 6

BEDROOM
8 × 8

CORRIDOR
4 × 17

ROOF

CLOSET
4 „ 6 × 5

CHIM.

CORRIDOR
3 × 12

CHIM.

CLOSET
7 „ 8 × 2,3

CHAMBER
13 × 16

CHIM.

ROOF

CHAMBER
13 × 16

CLOSET
6 „ 6 × 2,3

CHIM.

ROOF

ROOF

PLATE 15.

E. E. MYERS, Architect, Springfield, Ill.

Fig. 1. Front elevation.

Fig. 2. Side elevation.

Fig. 3. First floor plan, containing Hall, Parlor, Dining and Sitting-room, Kitchen and Pantry.

Fig. 4. Second floor, containing Guests' and Family rooms, Bath-room, two Bed-rooms and Servants' room.

Fig. 5. Basement plan. Scale sixteen feet to one inch. Cost $4,500.

PLATES 16, 17.

DESIGN FOR A DWELLING, STYLE FRENCH MANSARD.

BROWN & GRABLE, Architects, 307 Locust Street, St. Louis, Mo.

This house is suitable for a country or suburban residence. Can be built of brick or wood; cost built of merchantable brick and painted, $7,500.

Plate 16. Shows the front elevation and first story plan.

Plate 17. Plan of second story and attic.

Scale of elevation and plans eight feet to the inch.

PLATES 18, 19.

DESIGN OF SUBURBAN RESIDENCE.

E. E. MYERS, Architect, Springfield, Ill.

Plate 18. Front elevation and first floor plan.

Plate 19. Side elevation and second floor plan. Scale one-eighth of one inch to the foot.

This dwelling has been recently erected for W. B. Corneau, of Springfield, Ill. Cost $10,000.

Plate 15.

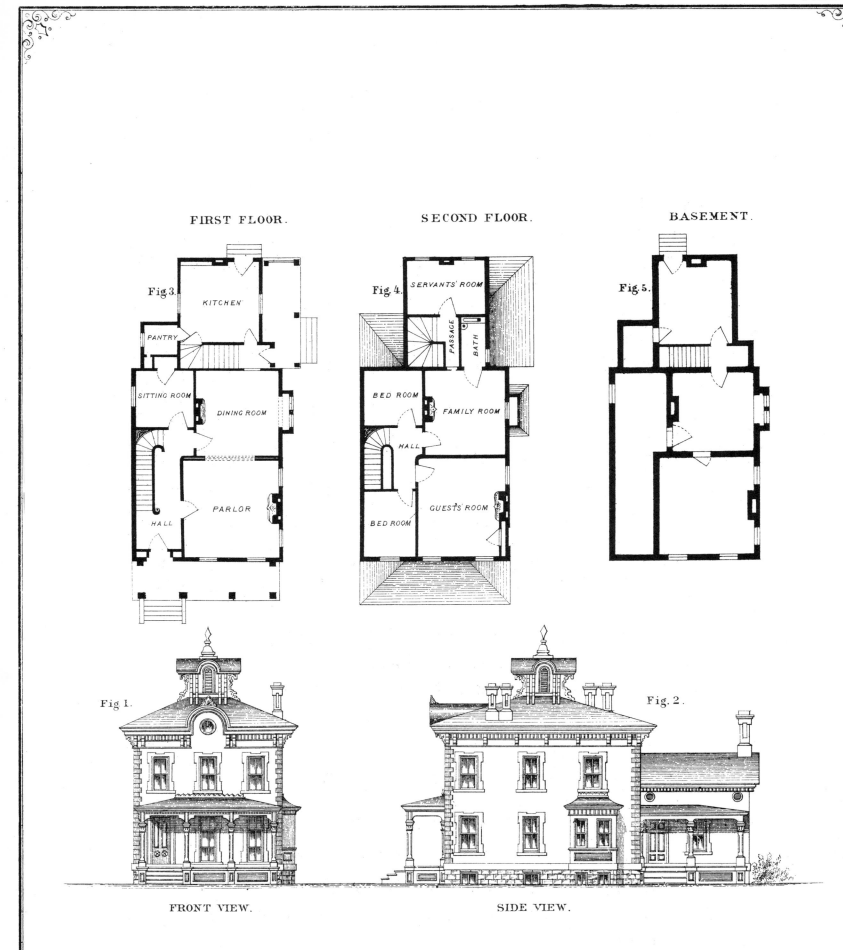

FIRST FLOOR.

Fig.3.

KITCHEN

PANTRY

SITTING ROOM

DINING ROOM

HALL

PARLOR

SECOND FLOOR.

Fig.4.

SERVANTS' ROOM

PASSAGE

BATH

BED ROOM

FAMILY ROOM

HALL

BED ROOM

GUESTS' ROOM

BASEMENT.

Fig.5.

Fig 1.

FRONT VIEW.

Fig. 2.

SIDE VIEW.

Plate 16.

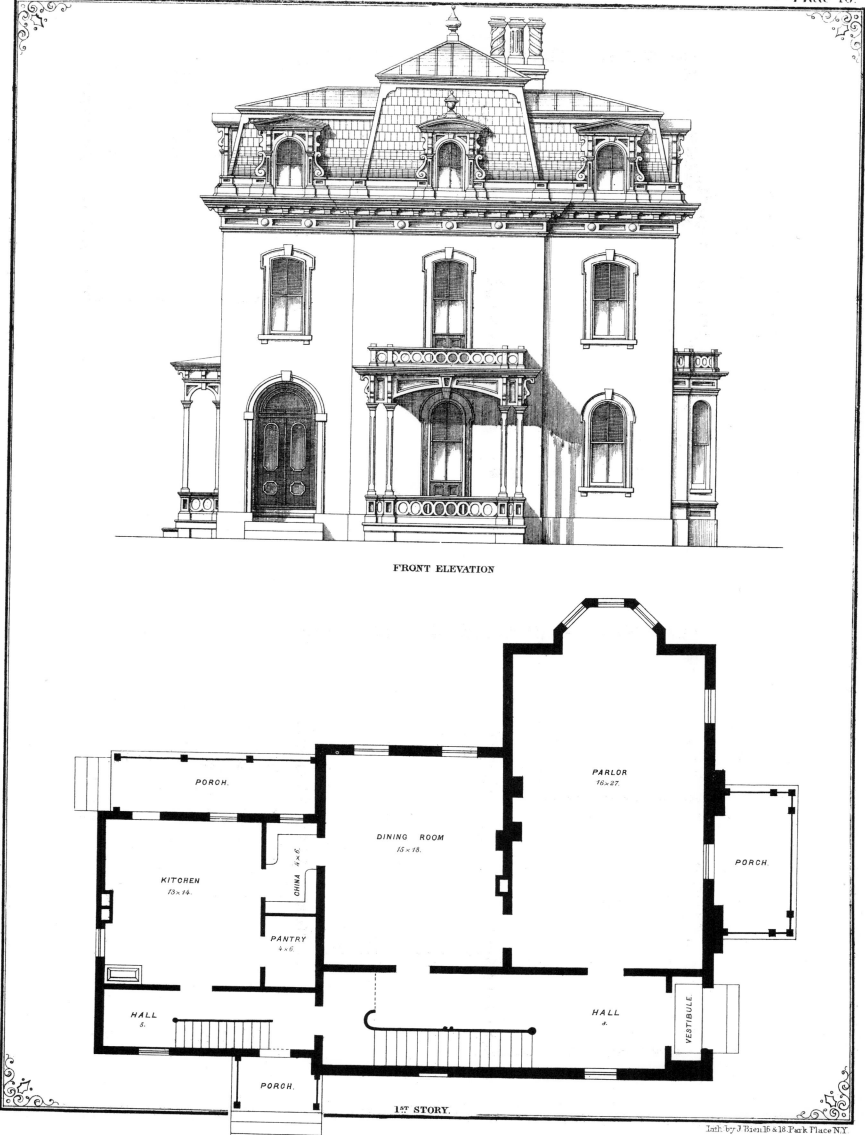

FRONT ELEVATION

PORCH.

PARLOR
16 × 27.

KITCHEN
13 × 14.

CHINA
4 × 6.

DINING ROOM
15 × 18.

PORCH.

PANTRY
4 × 6.

HALL
5.

HALL
8.

VESTIBULE

PORCH.

1ST STORY.

Lith. by J. Bien 16 & 18. Park Place N.Y.

Plate 17.

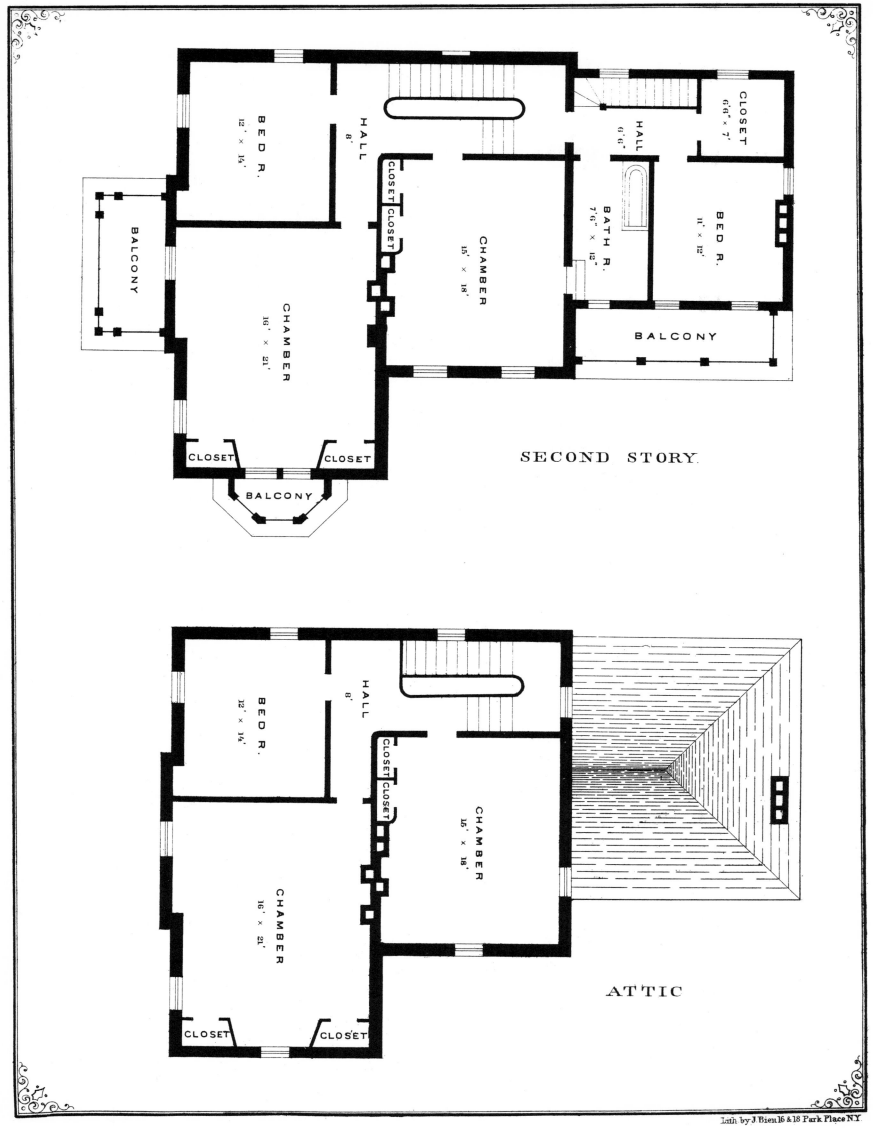

SECOND STORY.

ATTIC

Plate 18.

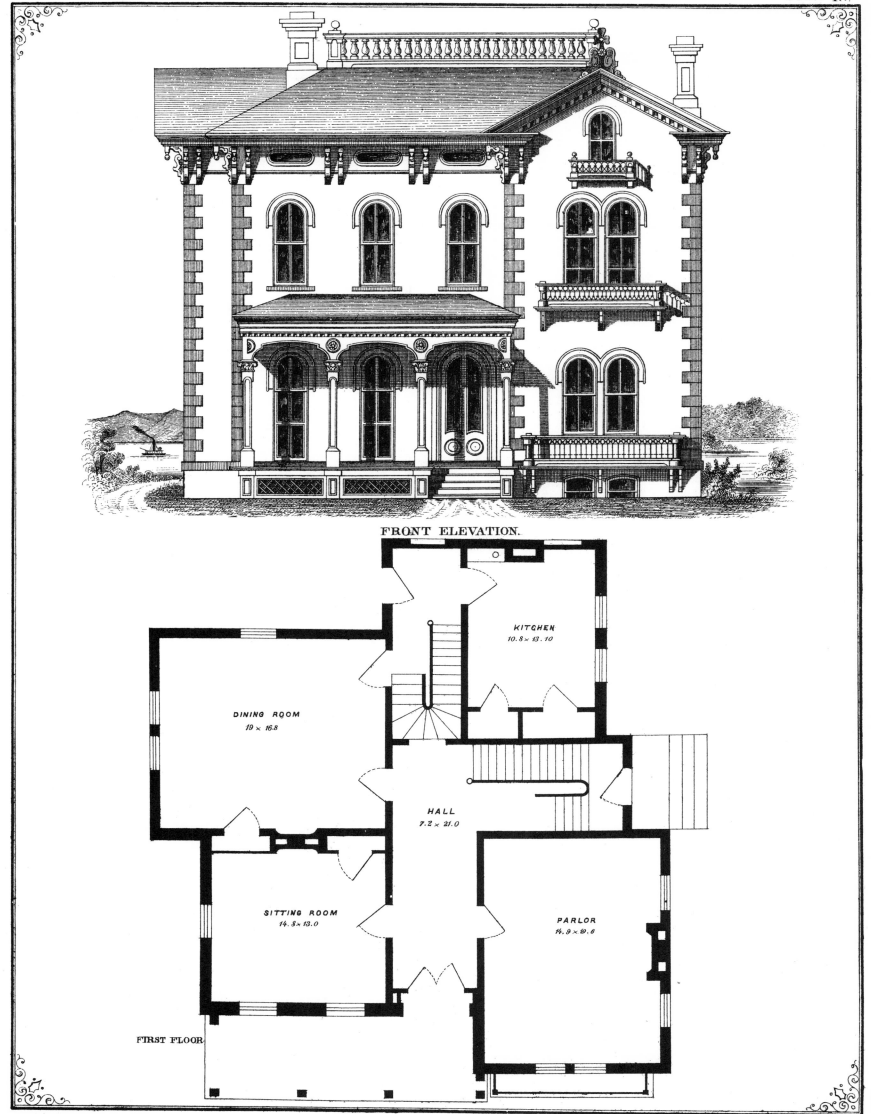

FRONT ELEVATION.

KITCHEN
10.8 × 13.10

DINING ROOM
19 × 16.8

HALL
7.2 × 21.0

SITTING ROOM
14.3 × 13.0

PARLOR
14.9 × 19.6

FIRST FLOOR

Plate 19.

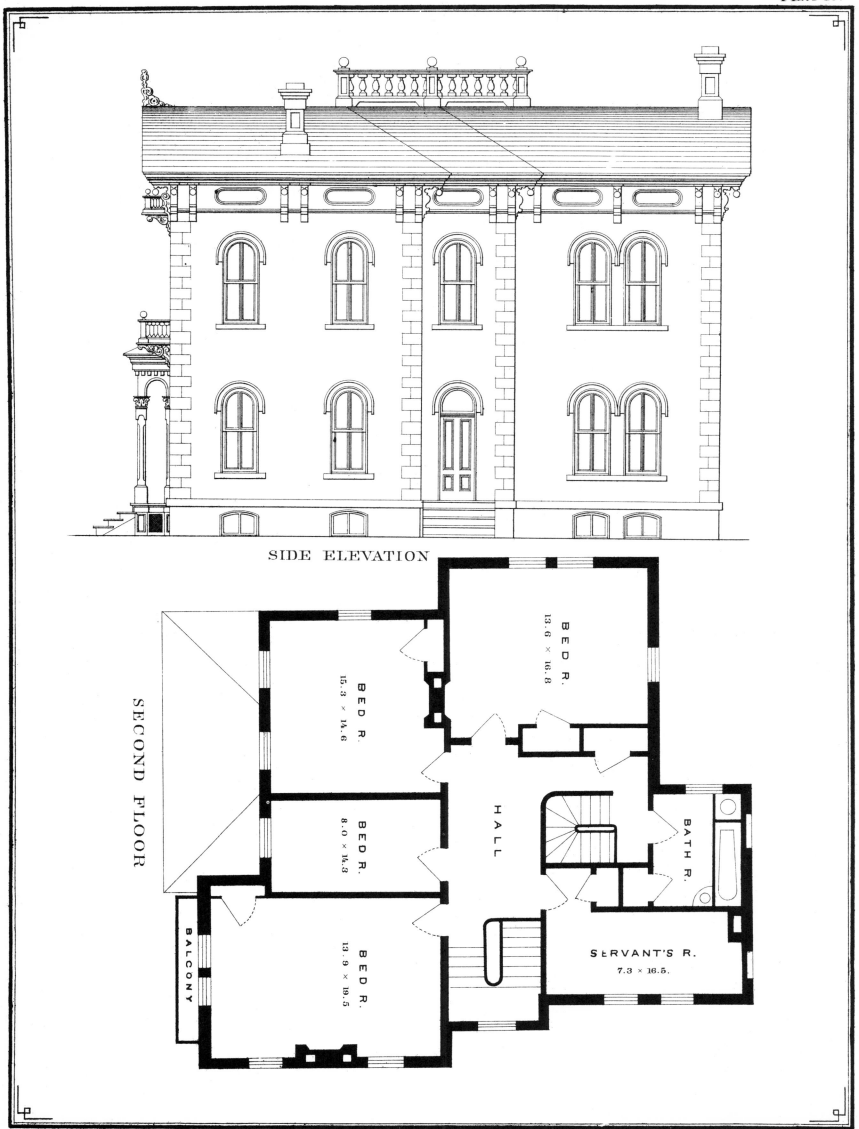

SIDE ELEVATION

SECOND FLOOR

BED R.
13.6 × 16.8

BED R.
15.3 × 14.6

BED R.
8.0 × 14.3

BED R.
13.9 × 19.5

BALCONY

HALL

BATH R.

SERVANT'S R.
7.3 × 16.5.

J. Bien, Lith.

Plate 20

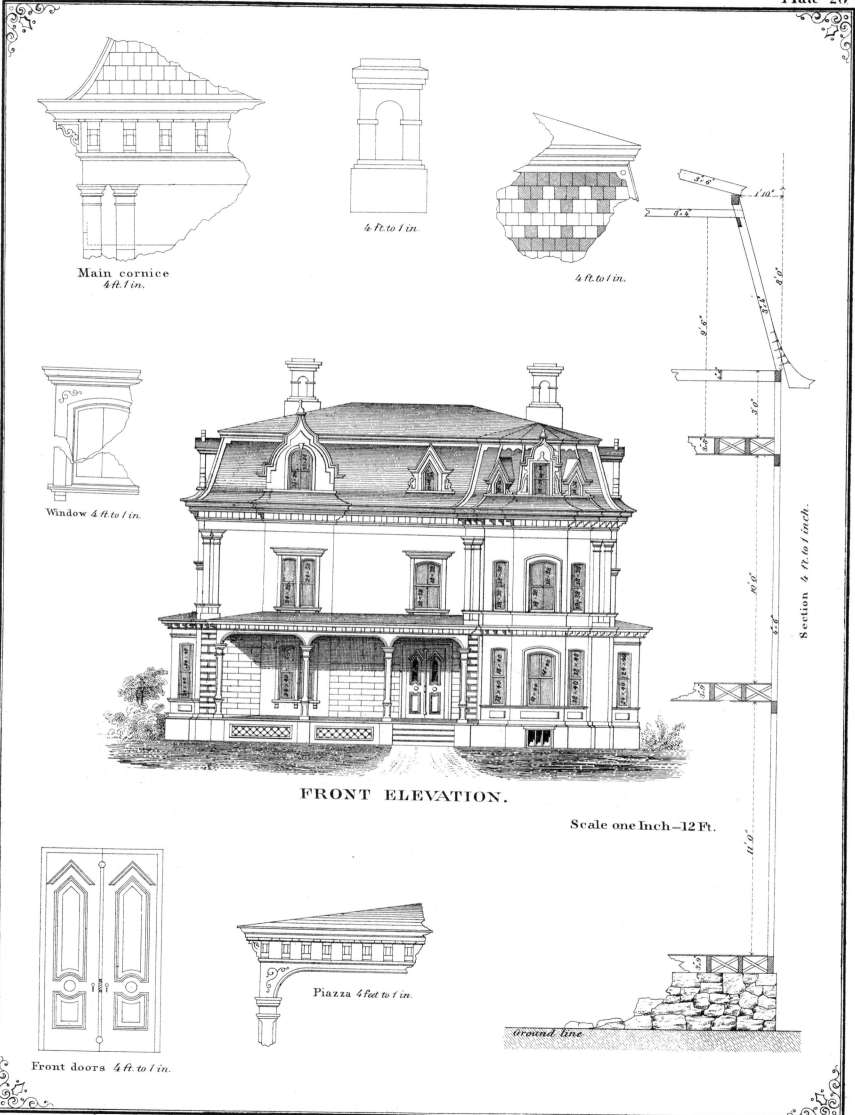

Main cornice
4 ft. 1 in.

4 ft. to 1 in.

4 ft. to 1 in.

Window 4 ft. to 1 in.

Section 4 ft. to 1 inch.

FRONT ELEVATION.

Scale one Inch—12 Ft.

Front doors 4 ft. to 1 in.

Piazza 4 feet to 1 in.

Ground line

Plate 21.

REAR ELEVATION

AND

GROUND PLAN

Scale 1-inch-12 ft.

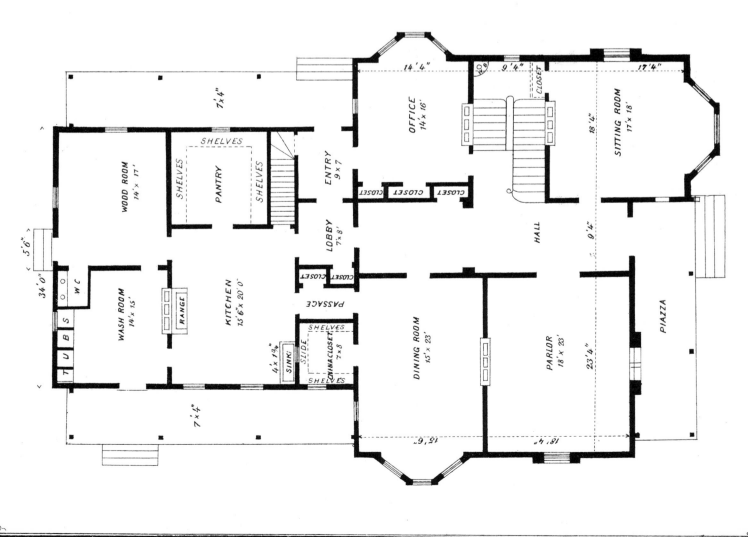

Plate 22.

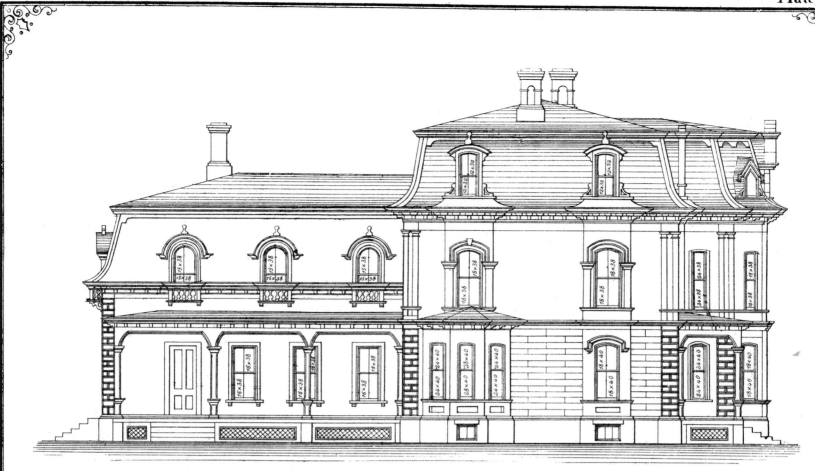

SIDE ELEVATION.

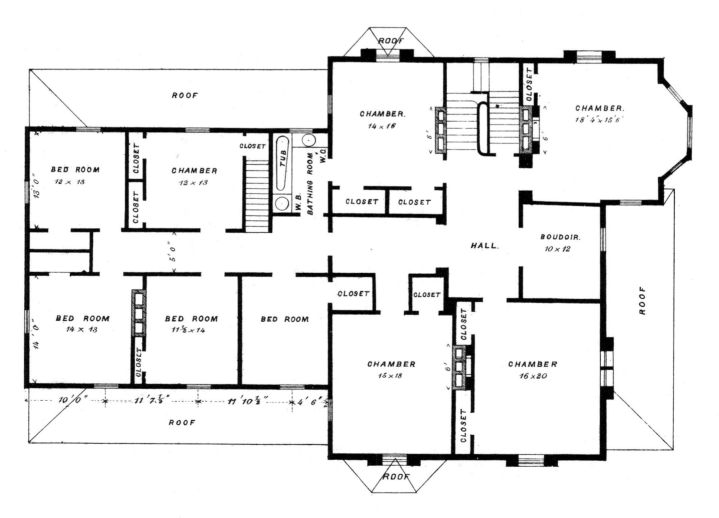

CHAMBER PLAN.

Scale 1 inch 12 feet

Lith by J. Bien 16 & 18 Park Place N.Y.

PLATES 20, 21, 22.

DESIGN FOR A FIRST CLASS DWELLING.

E. BOYDON & SON, Architects, Worcester, Mass.

Plate 20.   Front elevation.
Plate 21.   Rear elevation and ground plan.
Plate 22.   Side elevation and chamber plan.

This house has been built for Mr. J. A. Hovey, Ballston Spa, N. Y., and is one of the best residences in that section of the country.   The cost was $30,000.

Scale of plans and elevations one inch to twelve feet.

PLATES 23, 24, 25, 26.

DESIGN FOR A FARM HOUSE.

E. E. MYERS, Architect, Springfield, Ill.

Plate 23.   Shows the front view.
Plate 24.   First floor plan.
Plate 25.   Side view.
Plate 26.   Second floor plan.

This residence has been erected for Lewis Thomas, of Montgomery County, Ill., on a farm, containing 2,000 acres.   Cost $30,000.

Scale of elevations and plans three thirty-second of one inch to the foot.

PLATES 27, 28,

DESIGN FOR A HANDSOME SUBURBAN RESIDENCE.

F. Wm. READER, Architect, 307 Locust Street, St. Louis, Mo.

Plate 27.   Front elevation.
Plate 28.   Plans of Basement, first floor, second floor and attic: a, denotes range; b b, dumb waiters; c c c c, wash troughs; d d, waste soil pipes; e e e e, dining-room closets; f f, flues of range and furnace; g g, hot air flues; h h, hot air registers or grates; i i i i, ventilating ducts; k k k k, chamber closets; k, hall closets; k k, closet under stairs; l l, water-closets in basement; l l l, water-closets on second floor; m m m m m, wash-stands; m, hydrant and sink.

Scale of elevation, one-eighth of one inch to the foot; scale of plan, one-sixteenth of one inch to the foot.   Cost $21,000.

Plate 23.

FRONT VIEW

Scale of Details: ¼ of 1 inch to 1 foot.

Lith by J. Bien 16 & 18 Park Place N.Y.

Plate 24.

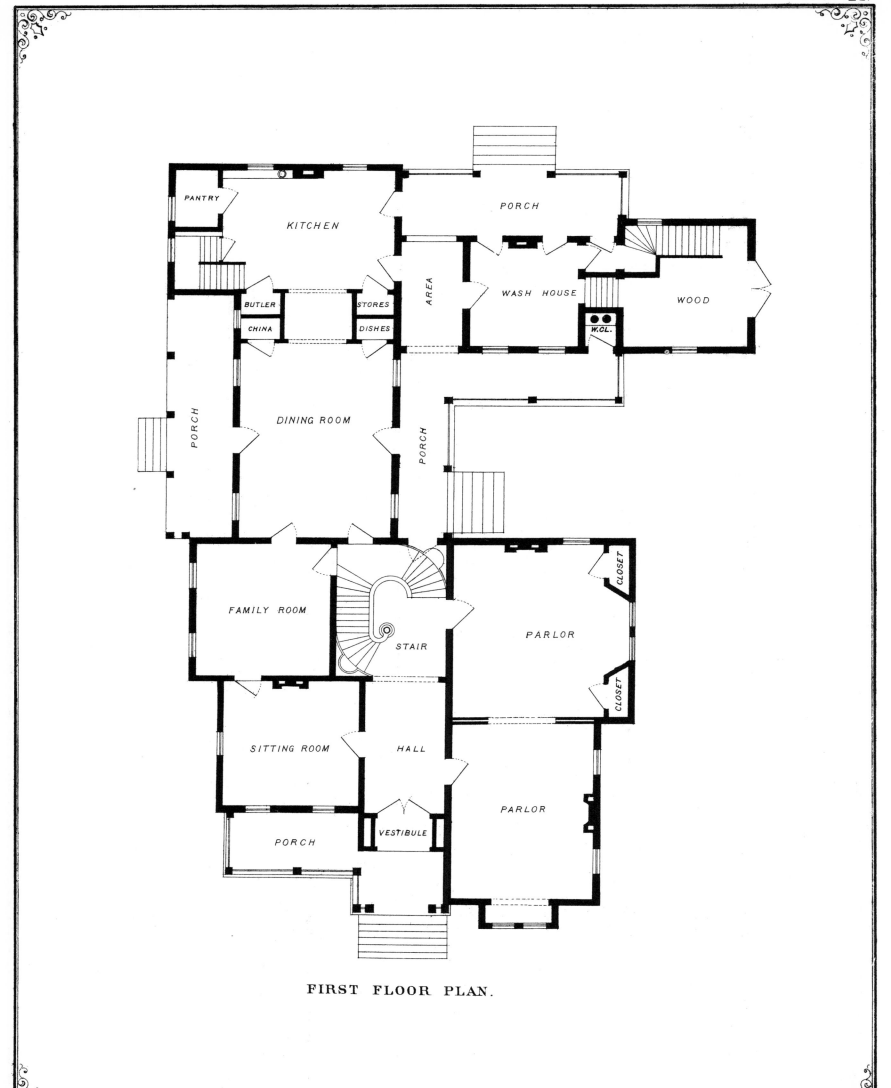

FIRST FLOOR PLAN.

Lith. by J. Bien 16 & 18 Park Place N.Y.

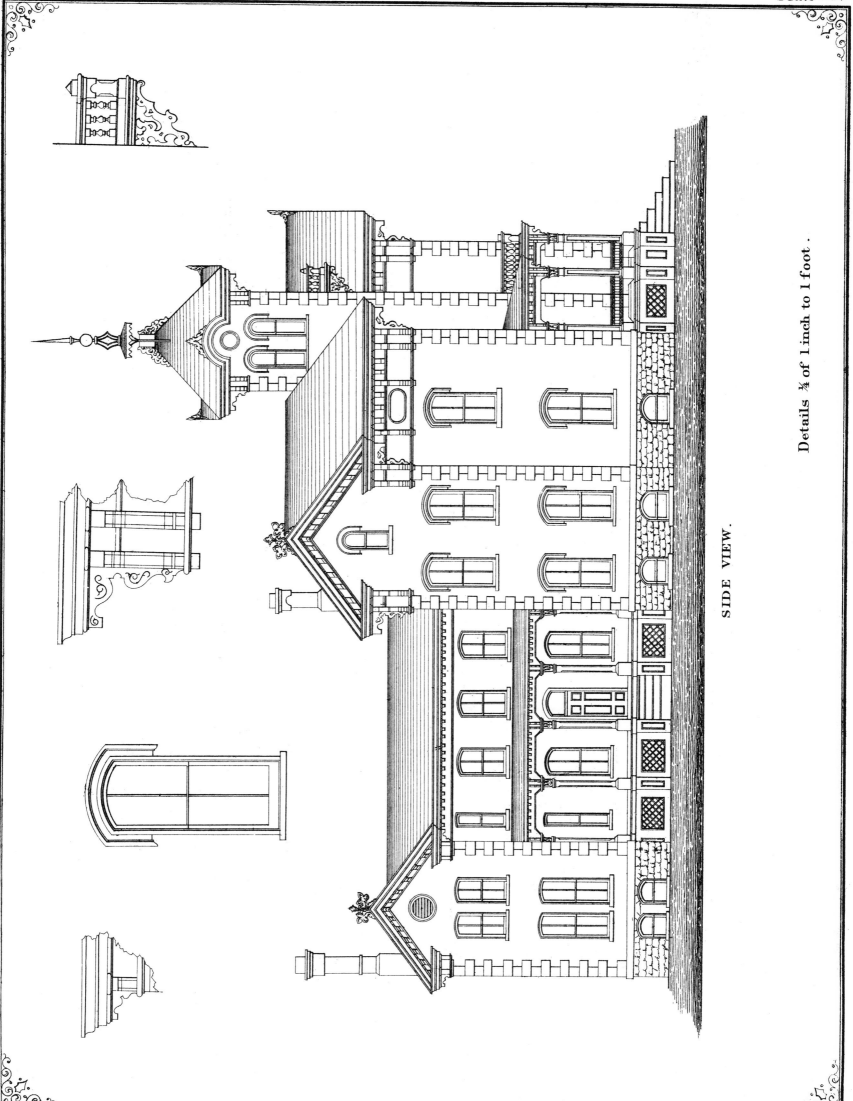

SIDE VIEW.

Details ¼ of 1 inch to 1 foot.

Lith. by J. Bien 16 & 13 Park Place N.Y.

Plate 26.

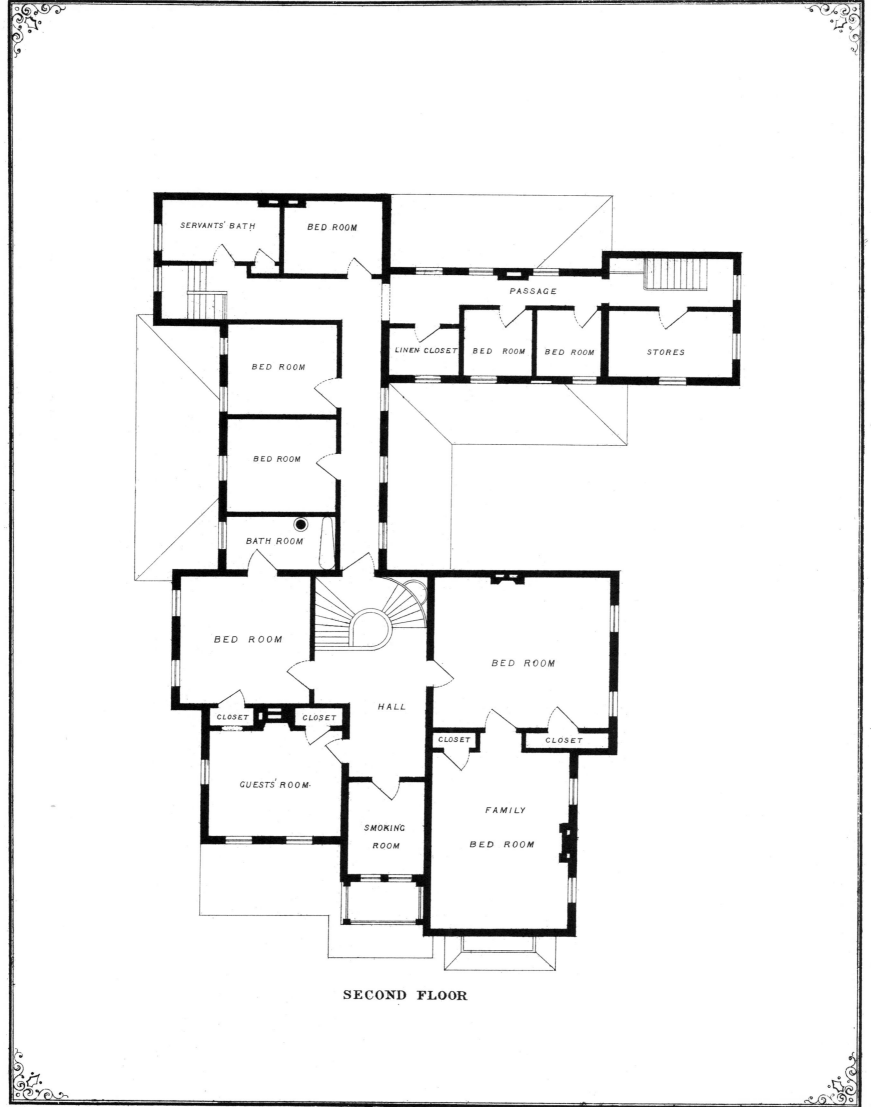

SERVANTS' BATH

BED ROOM

PASSAGE

LINEN CLOSET

BED ROOM

BED ROOM

BED ROOM

BED ROOM

STORES

BATH ROOM

BED ROOM

HALL

BED ROOM

CLOSET

CLOSET

CLOSET

CLOSET

GUESTS' ROOM

SMOKING ROOM

FAMILY

BED ROOM

SECOND FLOOR

Lith. by J Bien 16 & 18 Park Place N.Y.

Plate 27.

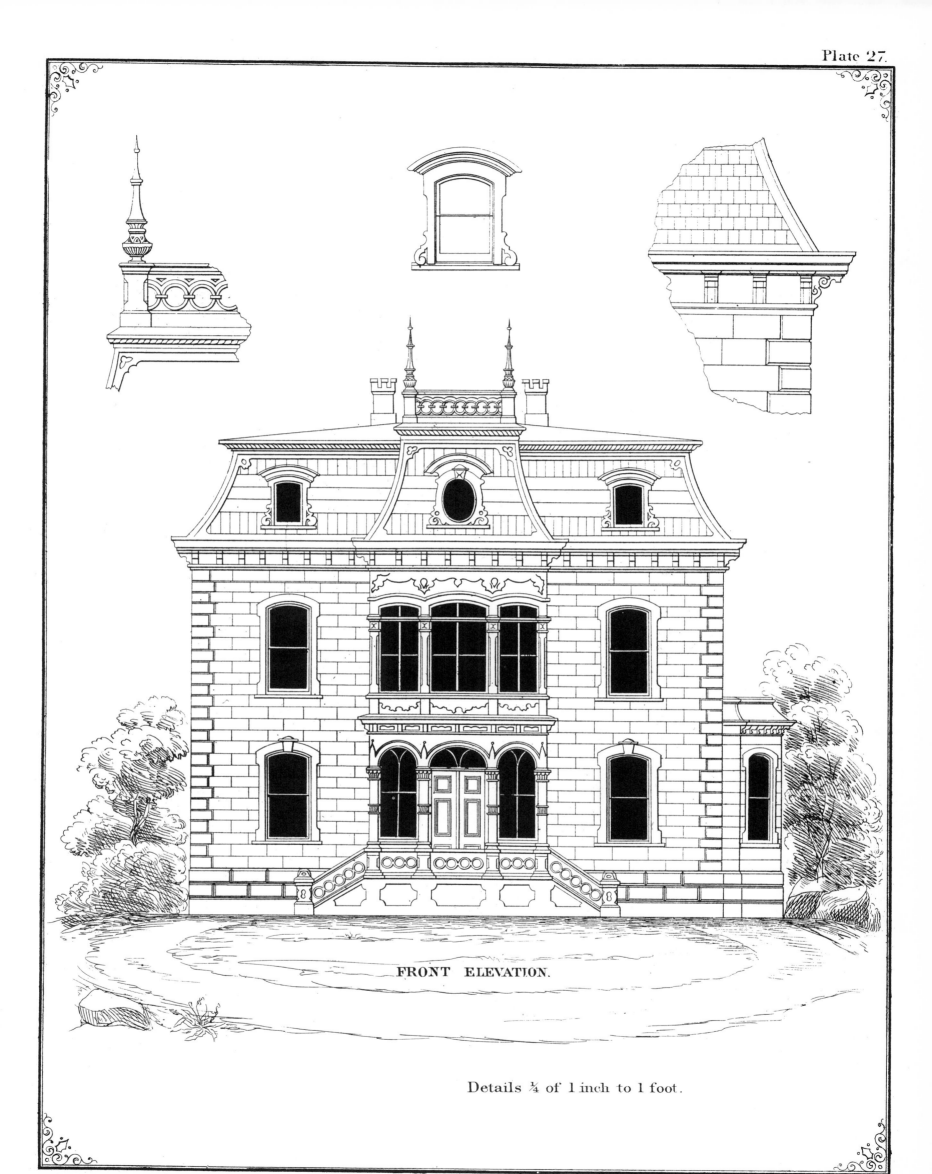

FRONT ELEVATION.

Details ¼ of 1 inch to 1 foot.

Lith by J Bien 16 & 18 Park Place N.Y.

Plate 28.

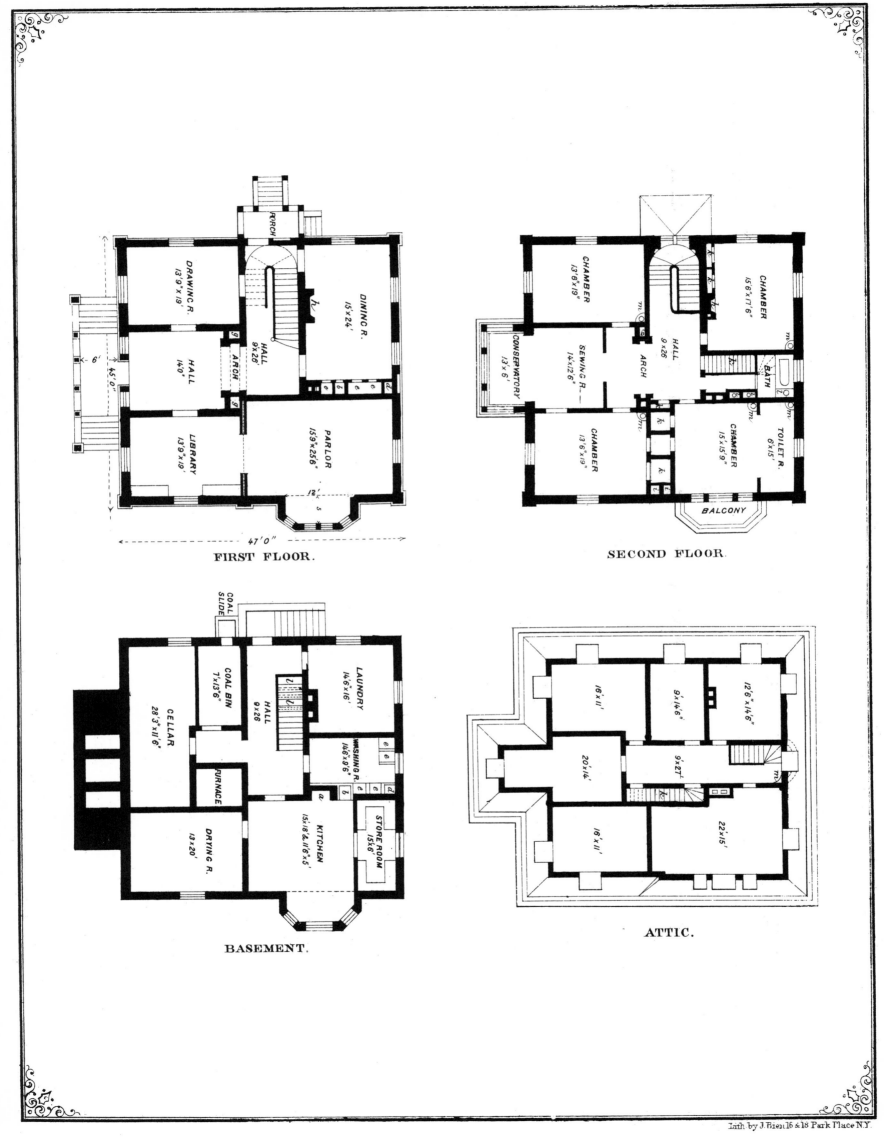

FIRST FLOOR.

DRAWING R. 13'9" x 19'

DINING R. 15' x 24'

HALL 9 x 26

HALL 14'0"

ARCH

LIBRARY 13'9" x 19'

PARLOR 15'9" x 25'6"

45'0"

6'

12'

47'0"

PORCH

SECOND FLOOR.

CHAMBER 13'6" x 19'

CHAMBER 15'6" x 17'6"

CONSERVATORY 13' x 6'

SEWING R. 14' x 12'6"

HALL 9 x 26

ARCH

BATH

TOILET R. 6' x 15'

CHAMBER 13'6" x 19'

CHAMBER 15' x 15'9"

BALCONY

BASEMENT.

CELLAR 28'3" x 11'6"

COAL BIN 7' x 13'6"

HALL 9 x 26

LAUNDRY 14'6" x 16'

WASHING R. 14'6" x 9'6"

FURNACE

DRYING R. 13' x 20'

KITCHEN 15' x 18' & 16' x 5'

STORE ROOM 15' x 6'

COAL SLIDE

ATTIC.

16' x 11'

9' x 14'6"

12'6" x 14'6"

20' x 14'

9' x 27'

16' x 11'

22' x 15'

Lith. by J. Bien 16 & 18 Park Place N.Y.

PLATE 29.

MODEL DESIGN FOR A CHEAP CITY DWELLING.

C. Bolin Stark, Architect, Philadelphia, Pa.

This Plate shows the front elevation, section and plans of a city residence of moderate cost. The basement has a kitchen, closet, and coal cellar; the first story ante-room, dining-room and closets; the second story contains library and parlor; third story—bed-room, dressing-room, bath-room and closet.

Scale—one-eighth of one inch to the foot. Cost, built of brick and plainly furnished, $2,000.

PLATES 30, 31.

PERSPECTIVE VIEW, FRONT ELEVATION AND PLAN FOR A FIRST-CLASS STABLE.

E. Boyden & Son, Architects, Worcester, Mass.

This stable has been recently erected for a gentleman at Worcester, Mass. The style of his residence is Elizabethan, and the stable is made to correspond. Cost $5,000.

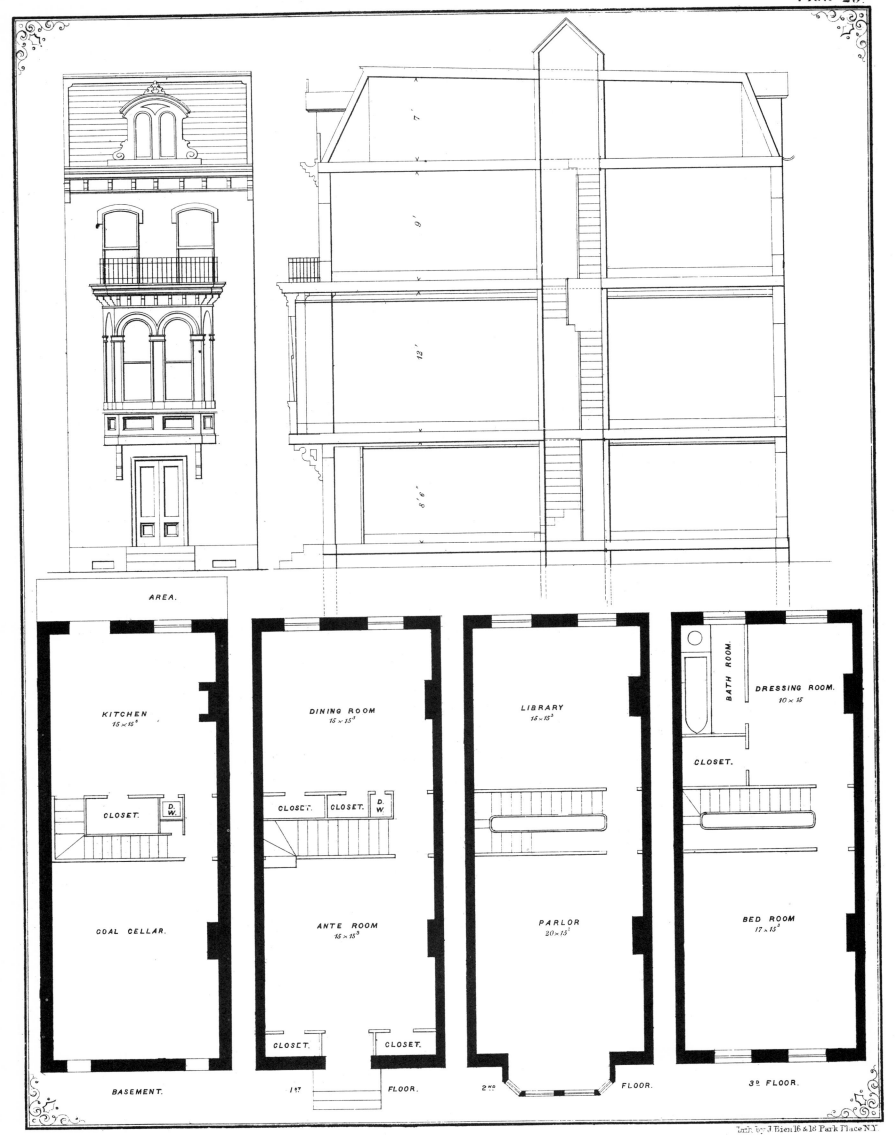

Plate 29.

AREA.

KITCHEN
15 × 15⁸

CLOSET. D.W.

COAL CELLAR.

BASEMENT.

DINING ROOM
15 × 15⁹

CLOSET. CLOSET. D.W.

ANTE ROOM
15 × 15⁹

CLOSET. CLOSET.

1ˢᵗ FLOOR.

LIBRARY
15 × 15⁹

PARLOR
20 × 15⁹

2ⁿᵈ FLOOR.

BATH ROOM.

DRESSING ROOM.
10 × 15

CLOSET.

BED ROOM
17 × 15⁹

3ᴰ FLOOR.

Plate 30.

Lith by J. Bien 16 & 18 Park Place N.Y.

Plate 31.

STABLE

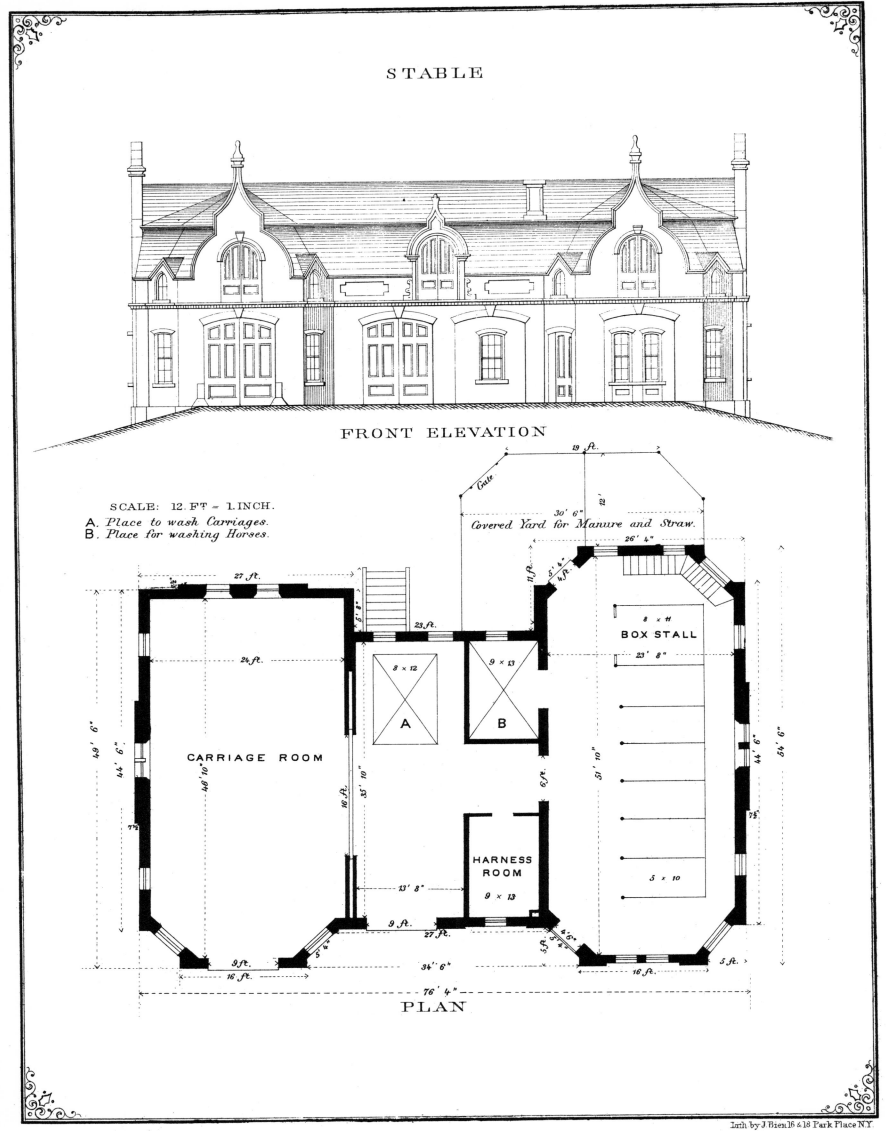

FRONT ELEVATION

SCALE: 12. FT = 1. INCH.
A. *Place to wash Carriages.*
B. *Place for washing Horses.*

Covered Yard for Manure and Straw.

CARRIAGE ROOM

BOX STALL

A

B

HARNESS
ROOM

PLAN

Lith. by J. Bien 16 & 18 Park Place N.Y.

PLATE 32.

ELEVATIONS AND PLANS FOR A CARRIAGE-HOUSE AND STABLE.

E. E. MYERS, Architect, Springfield, Ill.

Fig. 1. Front elevation.

Fig. 2. Side elevation.

Fig. 3. Plan of first floor.

Scale, eight feet to one inch.   Cost, built of brick and covered with slate, $2,700.

PLATE 33.

ELEVATION OF BLOCK OF TWO STORE-FRONTS.

E. E. MYERS, Architect, Springfield, Ill.

This block has been designed for the Hon. J. C. Conklin, of Springfield, Ill

Scale, one-eighth of one inch to the foot.   Cost $16,000.

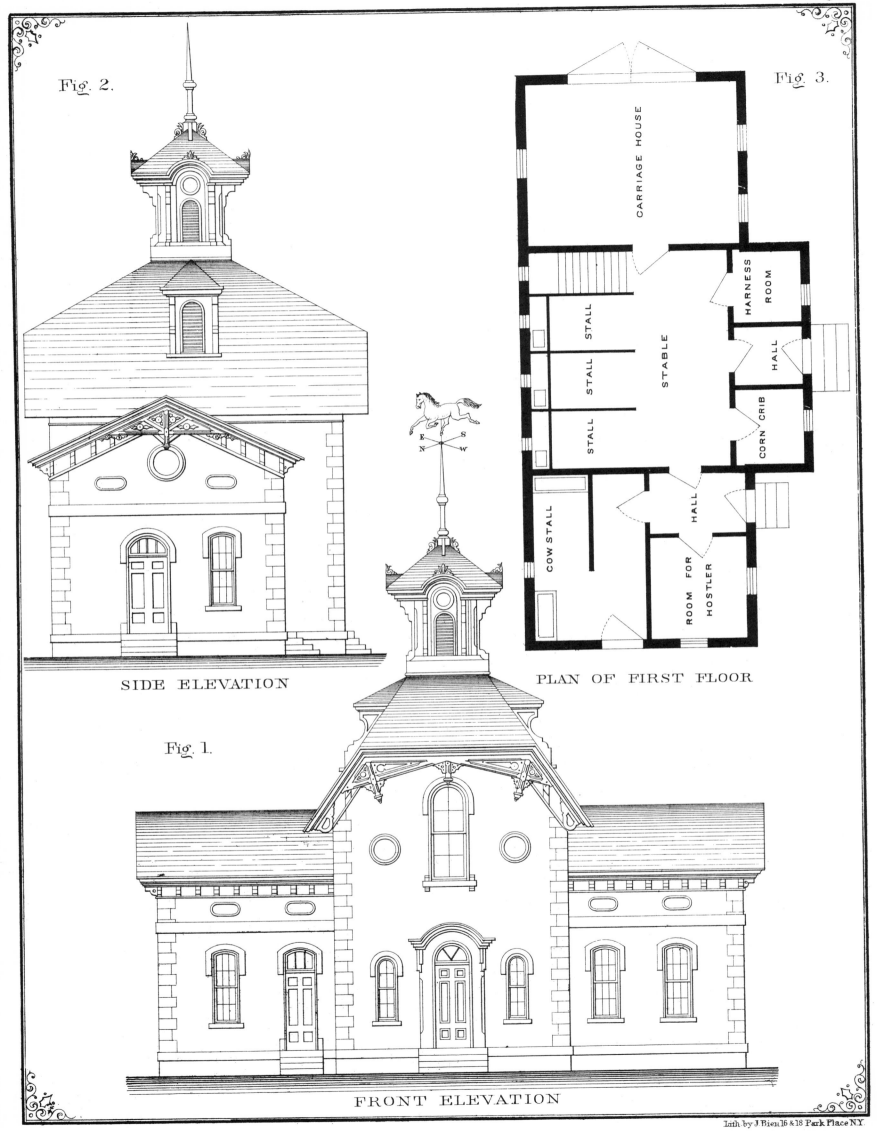

Plate 32.

Fig. 2.

Fig. 3.

CARRIAGE HOUSE

HARNESS ROOM

STALL STALL

STALL

STABLE

HALL

STALL

CORN CRIB

COW STALL

ROOM FOR HOSTLER

HALL

SIDE ELEVATION

PLAN OF FIRST FLOOR

Fig. 1.

FRONT ELEVATION

Plate 33.

CONKLING BLOCK SPRINGFIELD ILLINOIS 1869.

CONKLING BLOCK.

SCALE ⅛ INCH TO FOOT

Lith.by J.Bien 16 & 18 Park Place N.Y.

PLATE 34.

DESIGNS FOR STREET FRONTS FOR STORES.

G. B. Croff, Architect, Fort Edward, N. Y.

Design A, shows a store front prepared for Thomas Eldridge, to be built at Fort Edward.

Design B, has been executed in the village of Ballston Spa, N.Y., for John J. Luther, Esq.

A and B are drawn on the scale of three-sixteenth of one inch to the foot.

PLATE 35.

DESIGNS FOR FOUR STORES.

E. E. Myers, Architect, Springfield, Ill.

This block of stores is erected at Jacksonville, Ill.
Scale of elevation, one-eighth of one inch to the foot. Cost $30,000.

Plate 34.

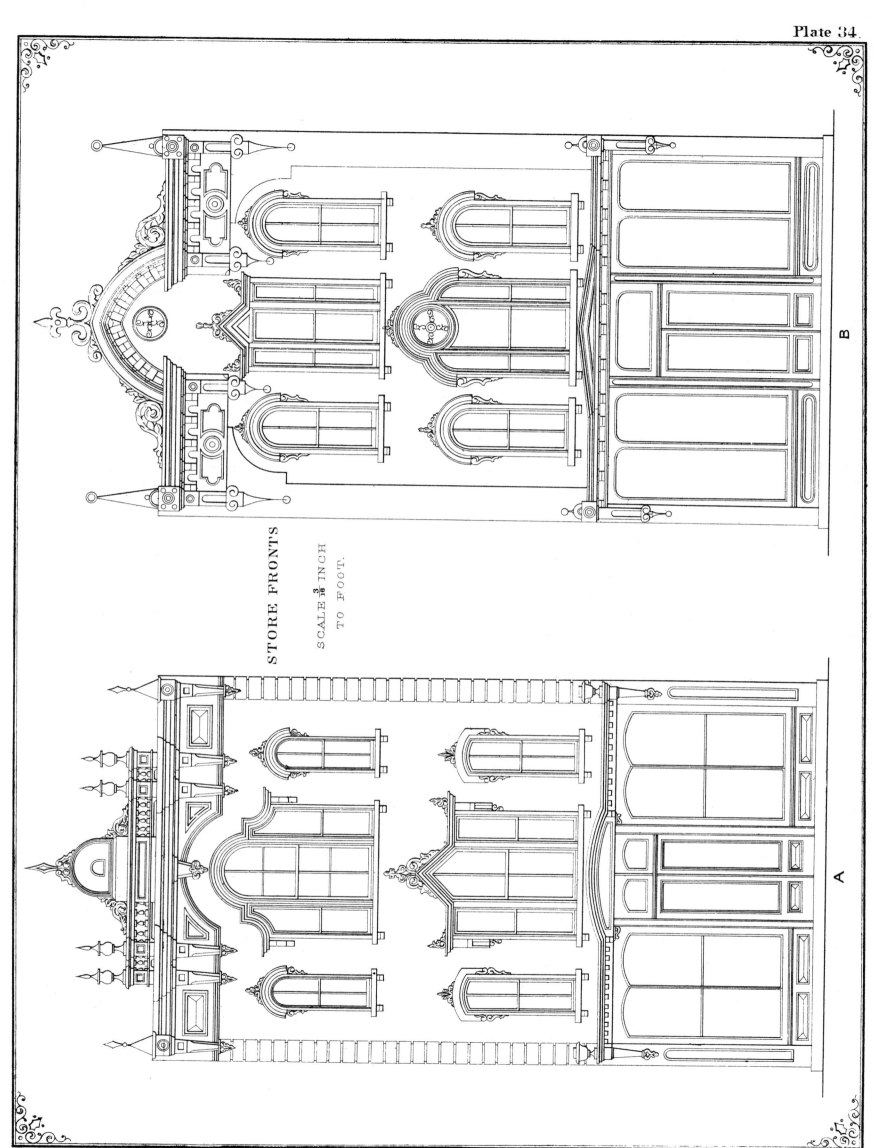

STORE FRONTS

SCALE $\frac{3}{16}$ INCH TO FOOT.

B

A

Lith. by J. Bien 16 & 18 Park Place N.Y.

Plate 35.

1868.

AYERS' BLOCK
JACKSONVILLE.

1868.

THE FRONT ELEVATION OF AYERS BLOCK AT JACKSONVILLE ILL.

PLATE 36.

DESIGN FOR A FRAME SCHOOL-HOUSE.

E. E. MYERS, Architect, Springfield, Ill.

This Plate shows the front elevation and plans for a two-story frame school-house, now being erected at Loami, Ill.

Scale of elevation, one-eighth of one inch to the foot; scale of plans, one-sixteenth of one inch to the foot. Cost $6,000.

PLATES 37, 38.

DESIGN FOR A BRICK SCHOOL-HOUSE WITH MANSARD ROOF.

THEO. F. LADUE, Architect, Lincoln, Ill.

Plate 37. Shows the front elevation and several details of a school-house now being erected at Lincoln, Ill. A, main cornice; B, tower cornice; C, top of steep roof; D, cornice of dormer windows.

Plate 38. First and third floor plan; the second story is arranged same as the first, with the exception of a school inspector's room over front hall. The building has two entrances, by front and rear; hall fifteen feet wide, with two stairways five feet wide, which communicate with all the rooms. There are four school-rooms on first, and second stories, with large wardrobes and teachers' closet for each room. The wardrobes are so arranged, that there need be no confusion coming in or going out. The third story contains a chapel and two recitation rooms. All the rooms are to be wainscoted with alternate ash and black walnut; and all windows are to be supplied with inside blinds. The walls are red brick trimmed with Milwaukee pressed brick.

The building will be heated and ventilated by Ruttan's system.

The basement is divided into fuel cellars, water-closets, etc.

Scale of plans and elevations, 1-12th of inch to the foot; scale of details, three-fourths of one inch to the foot. Complete cost $37,000.

Plate 36.

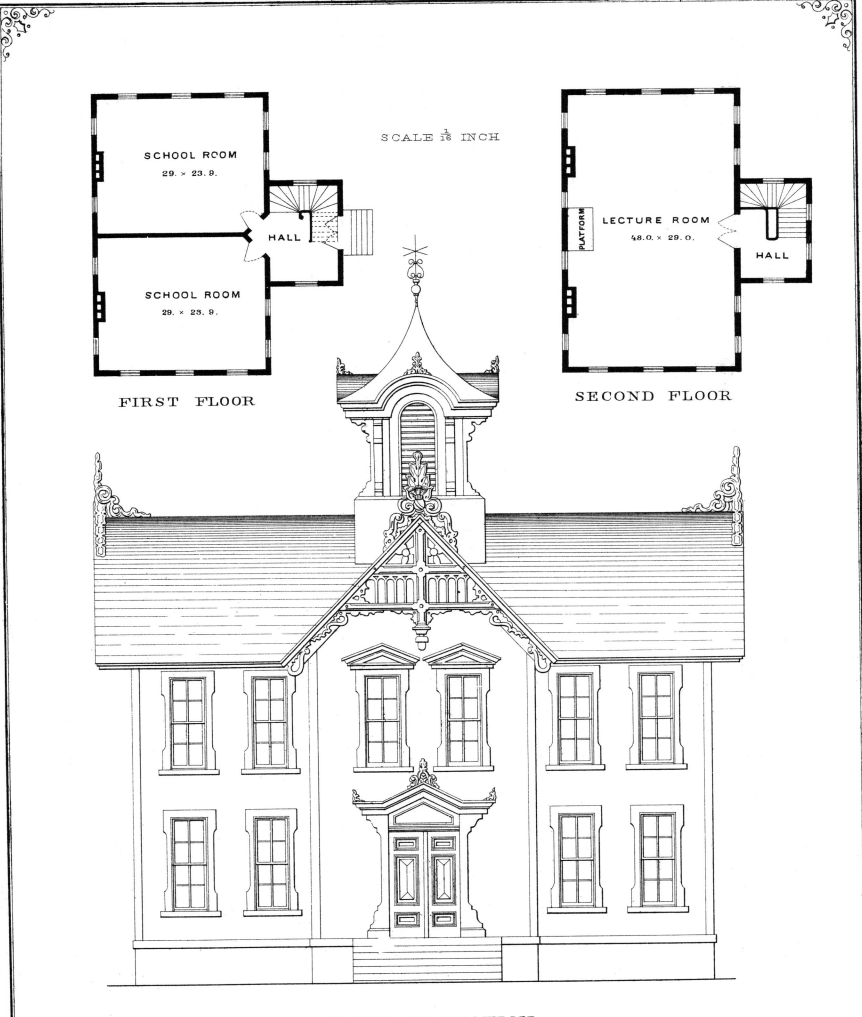

SCALE $\frac{1}{16}$ INCH

SCHOOL ROOM
29. × 23. 9.

HALL

SCHOOL ROOM
29. × 23. 9.

FIRST FLOOR

PLATFORM

LECTURE ROOM
48.0 × 29.0.

HALL

SECOND FLOOR

SCALE $\frac{1}{8}$ INCH TO FOOT.

FRONT ELEVATION

Lith. by J. Bien 16 & 18 Park Place N.Y.

Plate 37.

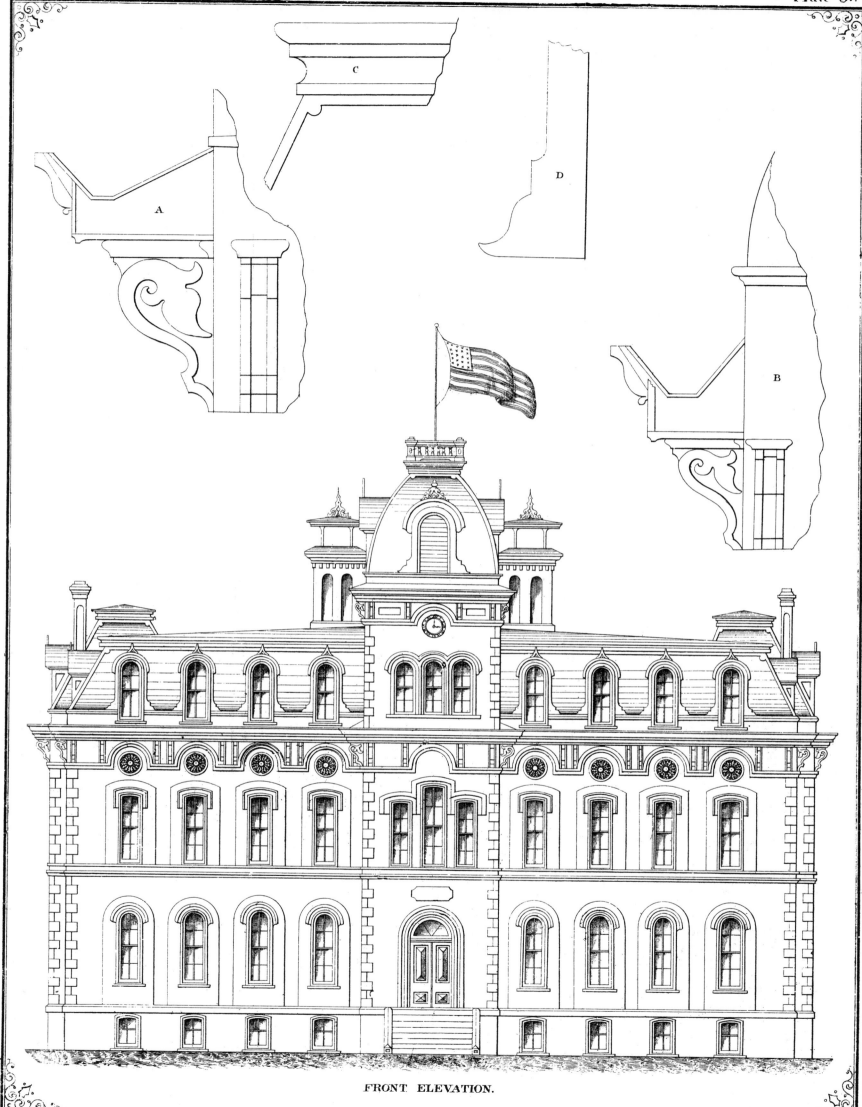

FRONT ELEVATION.

Lith by J Bien 16 & 18 Park Place NY.

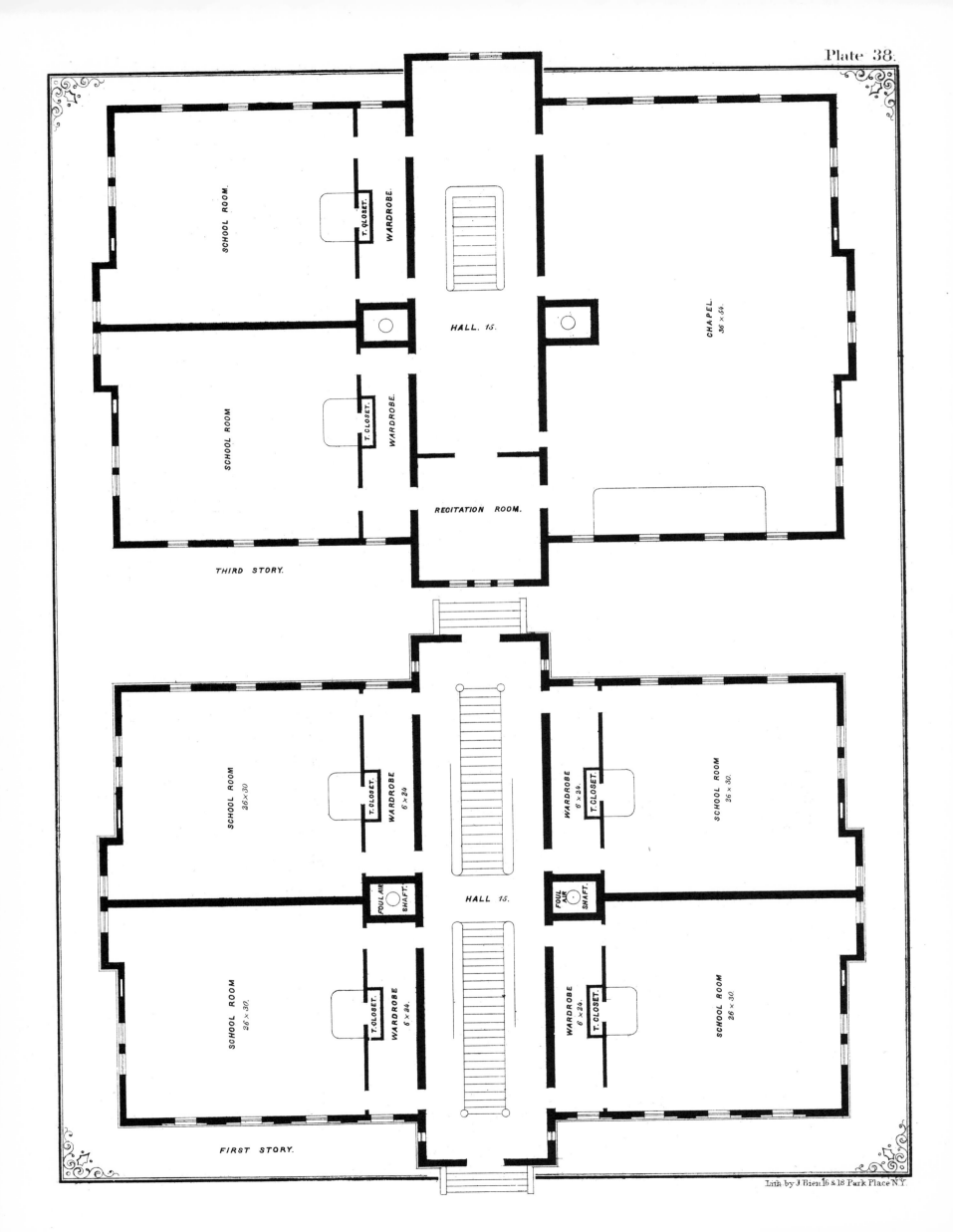

Plate 38.

SCHOOL ROOM.

T. CLOSET.

WARDROBE.

HALL. 15.

CHAPEL.
36 × 54.

SCHOOL ROOM

T. CLOSET.

WARDROBE.

RECITATION ROOM.

THIRD STORY.

SCHOOL ROOM
26 × 30

T. CLOSET.

WARDROBE
6 × 24

WARDROBE
6 × 24

T. CLOSET.

SCHOOL ROOM
26 × 30.

FOUL AIR SHAFT.

HALL 15.

FOUL AIR SHAFT.

SCHOOL ROOM
26 × 30.

T. CLOSET.

WARDROBE
6 × 24

WARDROBE
6 × 24

T. CLOSET.

SCHOOL ROOM
26 × 30

FIRST STORY.

Lith. by J. Bien 16 & 18 Park Place N.Y.

PLATES 39, 40, 41.

DESIGN FOR A SMALL CHURCH.

COCHRANE & PIQUENARD, Architects, 22, 23 & 24 Lombard Block, Chicago, Ill.

This design is now being erected in the flourishing city of Cheyenne, on the Union Pacific Rail Road. The style of architecture is what is known as modern Gothic. The building is thirty-two by forty-six feet, with a vestibule in front five and one-half by twenty-one feet, and corner tower ten feet square. The same will seat two hundred and ninety-six adults. The height of the interior is thirty-three feet to apex of ceiling, and that of spire eighty feet. The design is for a wooden structure upon a stone foundation.

Scale, eight feet to one inch. The cost will be $8,000.

Plate 39.

FRONT ELEVATION.

Lith by J. Bien 16 & 18 Park Place N.Y.

Plate 40.

SIDE ELEVATION.

Plate 41.

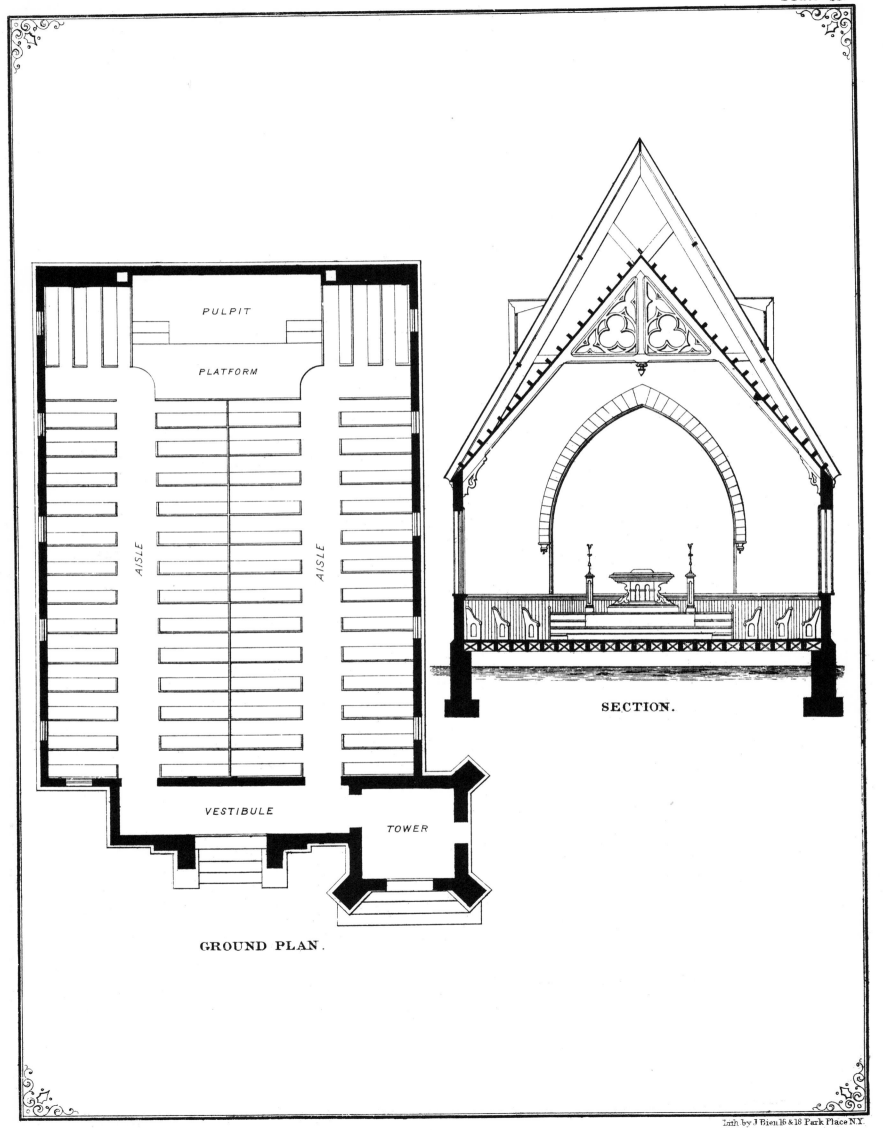

PULPIT

PLATFORM

AISLE

AISLE

VESTIBULE

TOWER

SECTION.

GROUND PLAN.

Lith by J Bien 16 & 18 Park Place N.Y.

PLATE 42.

DESIGN FOR A CHAPEL CHURCH.

LYMAN UNDERWOOD, Architect, 13 Exchange Street, Boston, Mass.

This Plate shows the front elevation and plan of a church edifice, with accommodations for about seven hundred persons. It is intended to be built of stone or brick, with cut stone dressings, although the same design might be carried out in wood. The entrances are numerous and conveniently arranged, as well as amply large. In the front is a vestibule nine feet wide, extending entirely across the building, containing four entrances to the audience room, as well as the stairs to the small gallery above. The audience room is sixty by seventy feet, with a chancel twenty feet wide at the end opposite the principal entrance, containing the pulpit or any other arrangements which denominational peculiarities might require. There are one hundred and thirty-six pews on the principal floor, with five sittings in each. The organ is on one side of the chancel and on the opposite is a minister's retiring room. Access to the audience room is also had through vestibules upon either side, and these vestibules also communicate with the vestry and committee rooms. The vestry is forty by forty-eight feet, the committee rooms each eighteen by twenty feet, communicating with each other by folding or sliding doors, and also with the vestry by the means of sliding sashes in addition to the ordinary doors. Above the committee rooms, and reached by an ample flight of stairs from the vestibule below is an additional room for the use of the ladies of the society. All of these various rooms would be abundantly lighted, and well ventilated. The expense of the building would of necessity vary very much with different localities, and with the amount of cut stone used upon the exterior; but under favorable circumstances it might be built of stone for about $18,000.

The elevation is drawn to a scale of sixteen feet to one inch, and the plan forty-eight feet to one inch.

Plate 42.

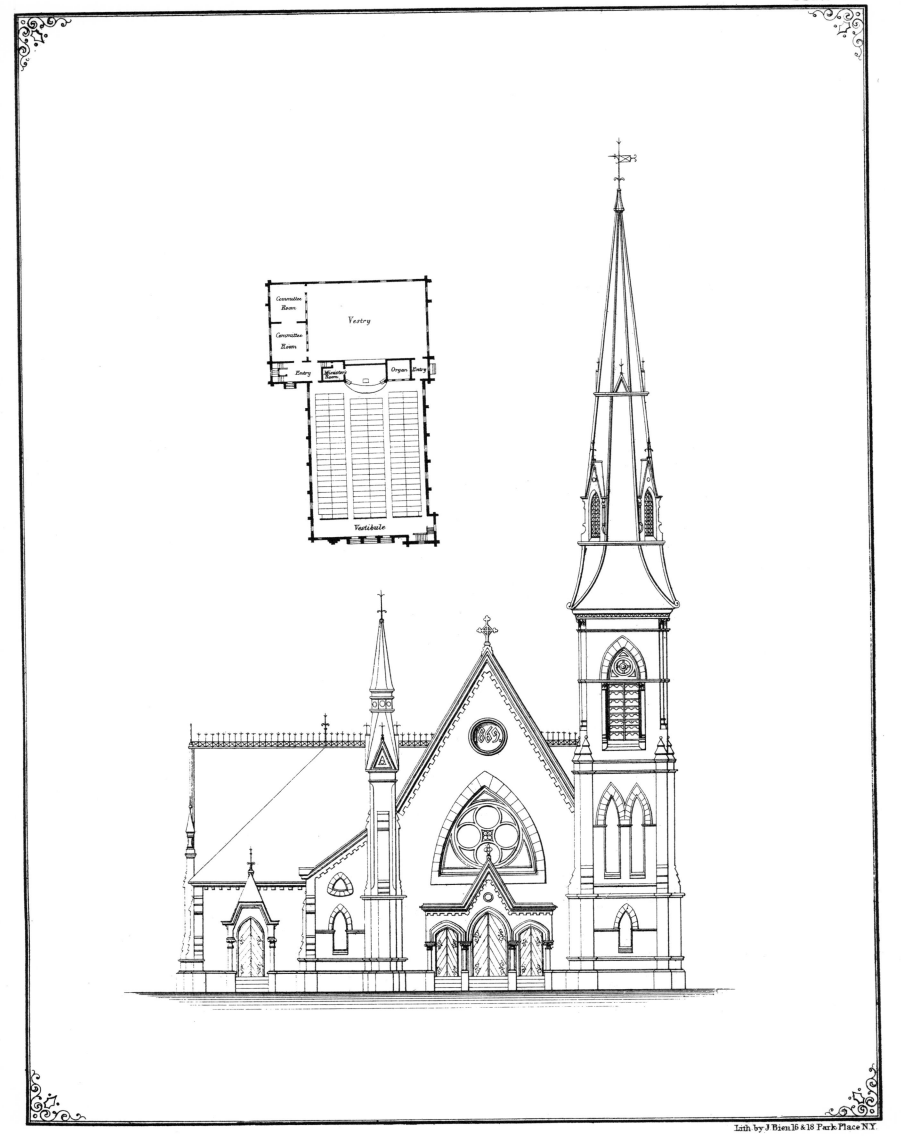

Committee Room

Committee Room

Vestry

Entry

Ministers Room.

Organ Entry

Vestibule

Lith. by J Bien 16 & 18 Park Place N.Y.

PLATES 43, 44.

DESIGN FOR A CHURCH.

DAVID S. HOPKINS, Architect, Grand Rapids, Mich.

Plate 43. Front elevation and basement floor.

Plate 44. Side elevation and audience floor.

A church after this design is built at Grand Rapids. It is much admired for its uniqueness and architectural beauty. It is architecturally Romanesque. The audience room is forty-six feet wide, sixty feet long, and thirty-five feet high to ceiling, with gallery over front vestibule, extending around from transept to transept. The audience room will seat six hundred and the gallery two hundred persons. The front vestibule is thirteen feet wide by forty-six feet long. Rear vestibule, fourteen feet square. Rostrum, eleven by thirteen feet. Choir, nine by eleven feet. Organ recess, ten by eleven feet. The basement is twelve feet in clear. Lecture-room, about the same size as audience-room, with two class-rooms in front, with sliding doors to the same into lecture-room. Library and parlor in rear. Outside dimensions, one hundred and two feet long by sixty-four feet wide, including the projection of the steeple spire, one hundred and fifty-five feet high. It is built of white brick with brown sandstone trimmings. Cost $40,000.

Plate 43.

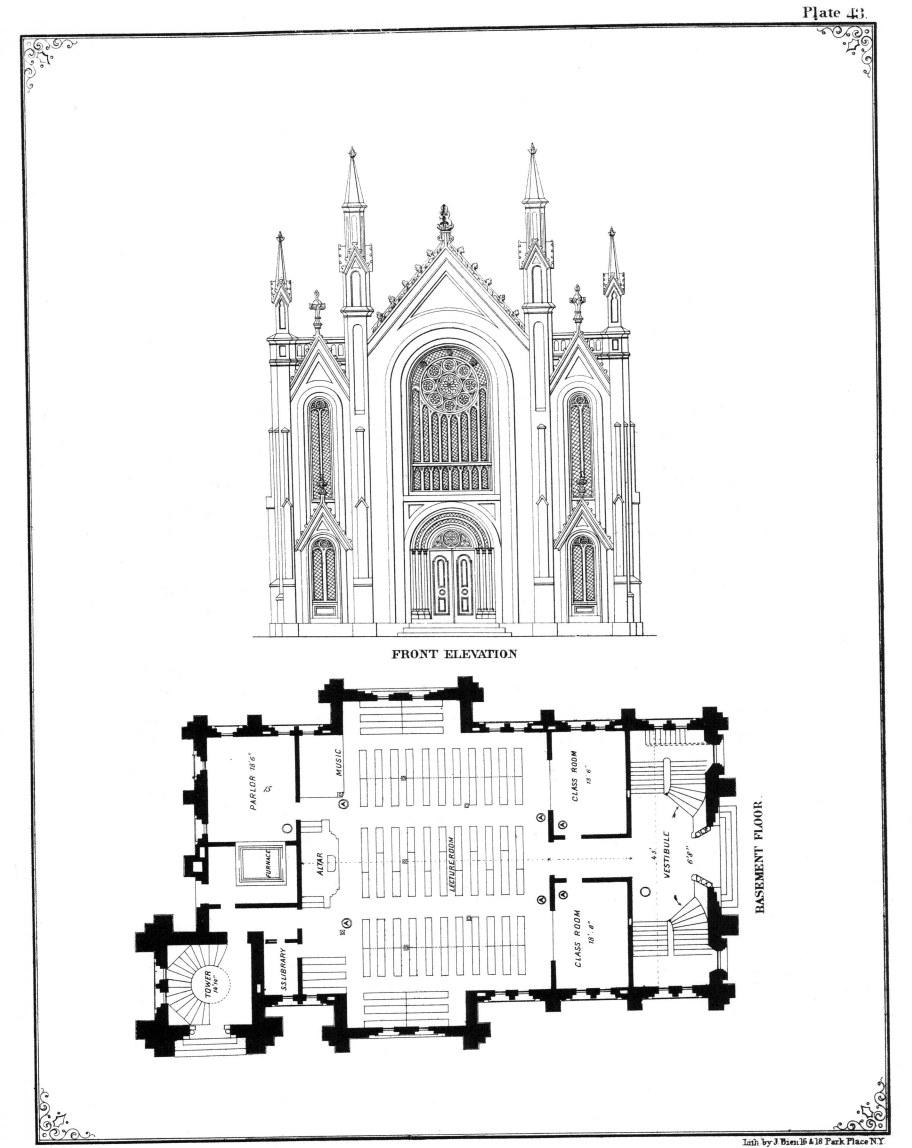

FRONT ELEVATION

BASEMENT FLOOR.

Plate 44.

SIDE ELEVATION.

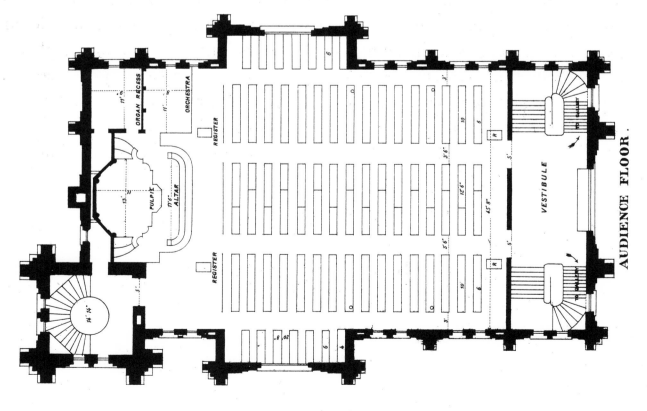

PLATES 45, 46, 47, 48.

DESIGN FOR A FIRST-CLASS COURT-HOUSE.

E. E. MYERS, Architect, Springfield, Ill.

Plate 45. Front elevation.
Plate 46. First floor plan.
Plate 47. Side elevation.
Plate 48. Second floor plan.

This design has been recently executed at Carlinville, Macoupin Co., Ill., and so far as known, it is strictly the only fire-proof building in the country, and is considered the finest county court-house in the United States.   The exterior is Athens marble.   The windows and door-frames, and the book-cases are all iron.   The floors are marble.   The interior of the court-room is lined with cast-iron painted in fresco and bronze.   The Judge's stand is of granite.   The length of building, two hundred and twenty-five feet; width, eighty-six feet; height from ground, eighty-six feet; height of lantern on dome, one hundred and eighty-six feet nine inches.   The building throughout is of the finest and best material, no cost having been spared to make it perfect in all its parts.

Scale of elevation and plans, one-eighteenth of one inch to the foot.

Plate 45.

FRONT VIEW
OF MACOUPIN COUNTY COURT HOUSE.

Scale ¹⁄₁₆ Inch to Foot.

Lith by J.Bien 16 & 18 Park Place N.Y.

Plate 46.

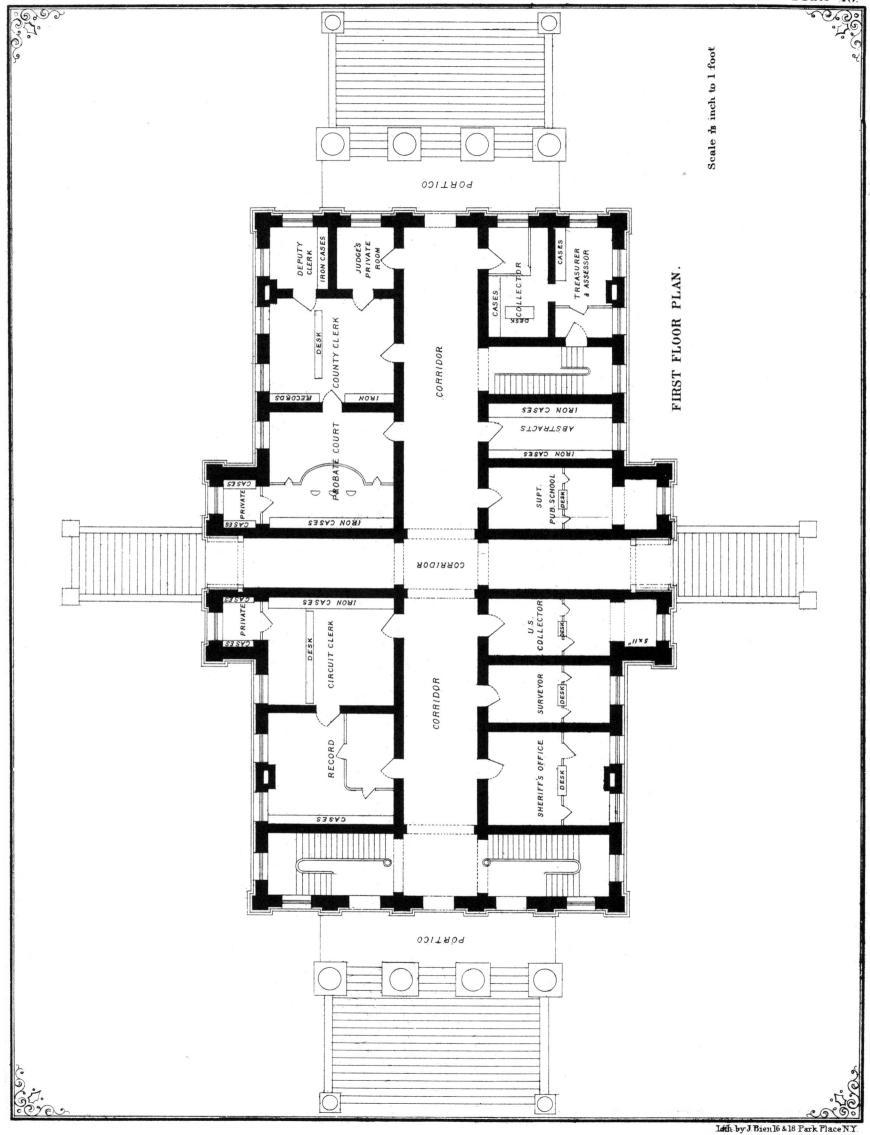

FIRST FLOOR PLAN.

Scale ⅛ inch to 1 foot

Plate 47.

SIDE VIEW of MACOUPIN COUNTY COURT HOUSE.

Scale ⅛ inch to 1 foot.

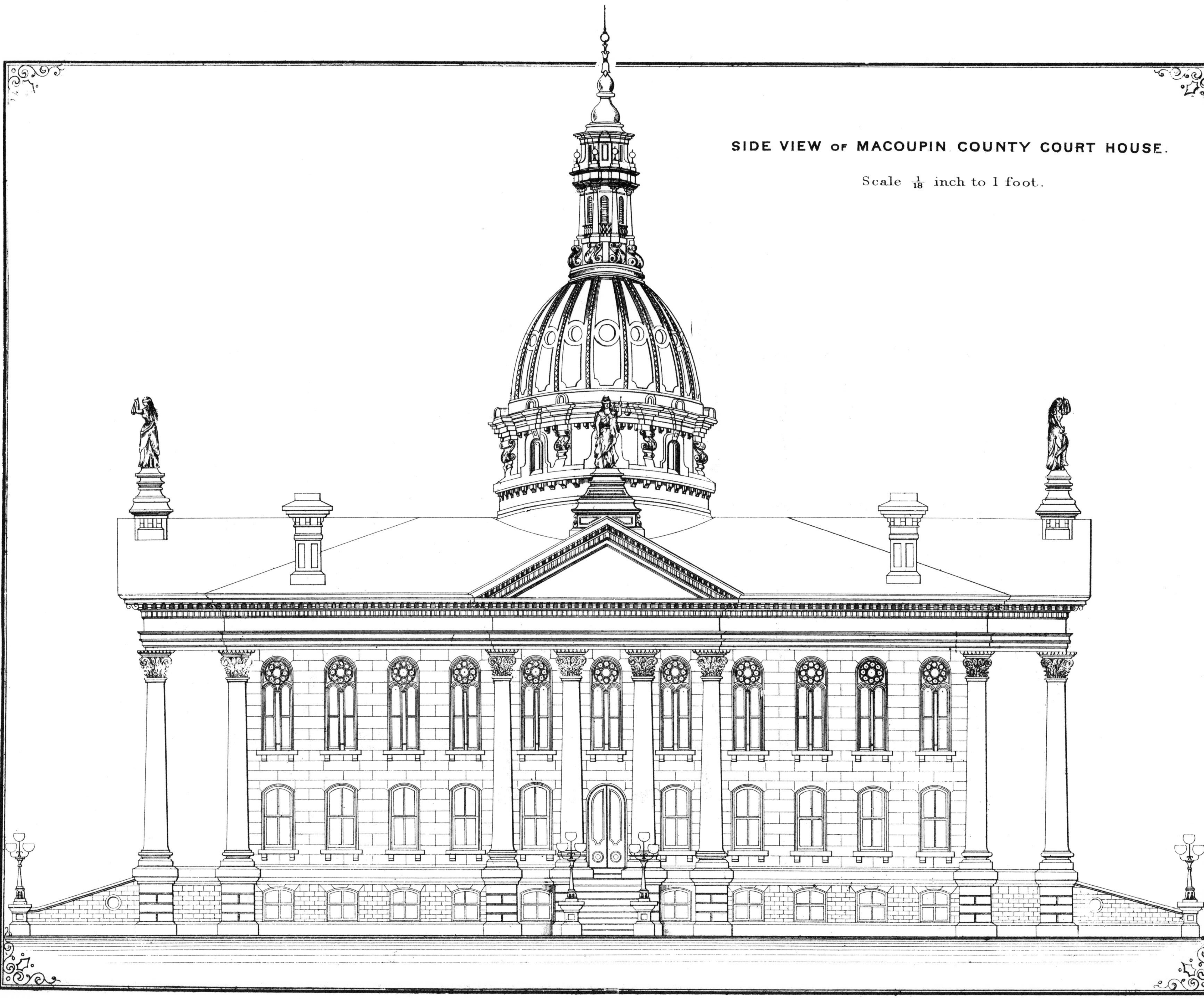

Lith. by J. Bien 16 & 18 Park Place N.Y.

Plate 48.

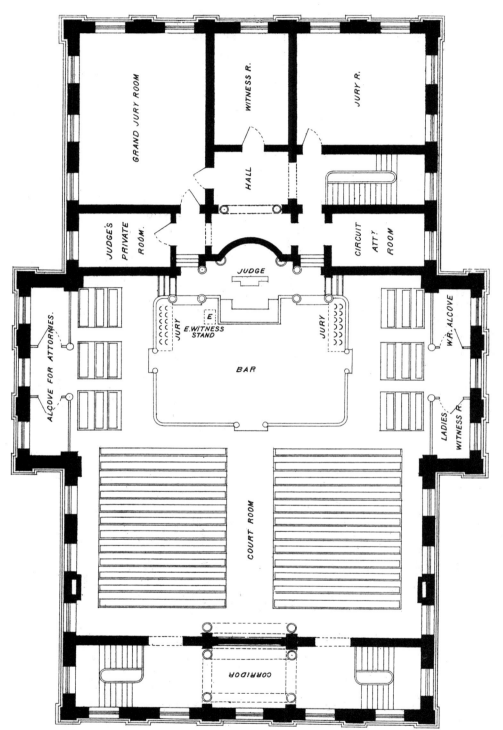

PLATES 49, 50, 51.

DESIGN OF BAY COUNTY COURT-HOUSE, BAY CITY, MICH.

Cyrus K. Porter, Architect, Buffalo, N.Y.

Plate 49. Fig. 1, Front elevation.

Fig. 2. Plan of first floor. A, Hall with stairways at each end of main hall, leading to court-rooms above; B, Supervisors' room; C, County clerk's office, with private office; E, D, County treasurer's office, with private office; G, Sheriff's office; H, Clerk of court's office; B, might be used as office of Probate Judge, as either C or D would answer for Board of Supervisors. The rooms in this story are all fourteen feet high in the clear. Safes, I, I, are provided for the offices.

Plate 50. Fig. 3, Side elevation.

Fig. 4. K, Court-room, forty-eight by seventy-one feet, and twenty-two feet high in clear; L, is the Bar containing seats for the judges, jury, and officers of the court; M, Witnesses' waiting-room, with water-closet; N, Counsel room and library; O and P, Jury rooms, one of which is designed to be used as a judge's dressing or retiring-room; they are both supplied with private entrances, water-closets, etc. These rooms are twelve feet high in clear. L, is a stairway leading to an attic above, and from thence to the top of the dome.

The drawings on Plates 49 and 50 are to a scale of sixteen feet to one inch.

Plate 51. Shows the most important details, drawn to a scale of one-half inch to the foot. A, B and F, Portions of dormer windows; C, Main cornice; D, Dome cornice; E, Base and plinth of dome; G, Cornice at angle of roof; H, Cornice of railing around top of dome; L, Chimney top; M and N, Inside finish, one-fourth full size; O, Stairway; P, Wainscoting of court-room; Q and R, Sections of doors, one-half inch to one foot.

The building has a basement of Kingston stone, the superstructure of yellow brick, with sandstone dressings. It is warmed with steam and lighted with gas. The cost was about $42,000, finished in the most substantial manner. Geo. Watkins, of Bay City, was the builder.

Plate 49.

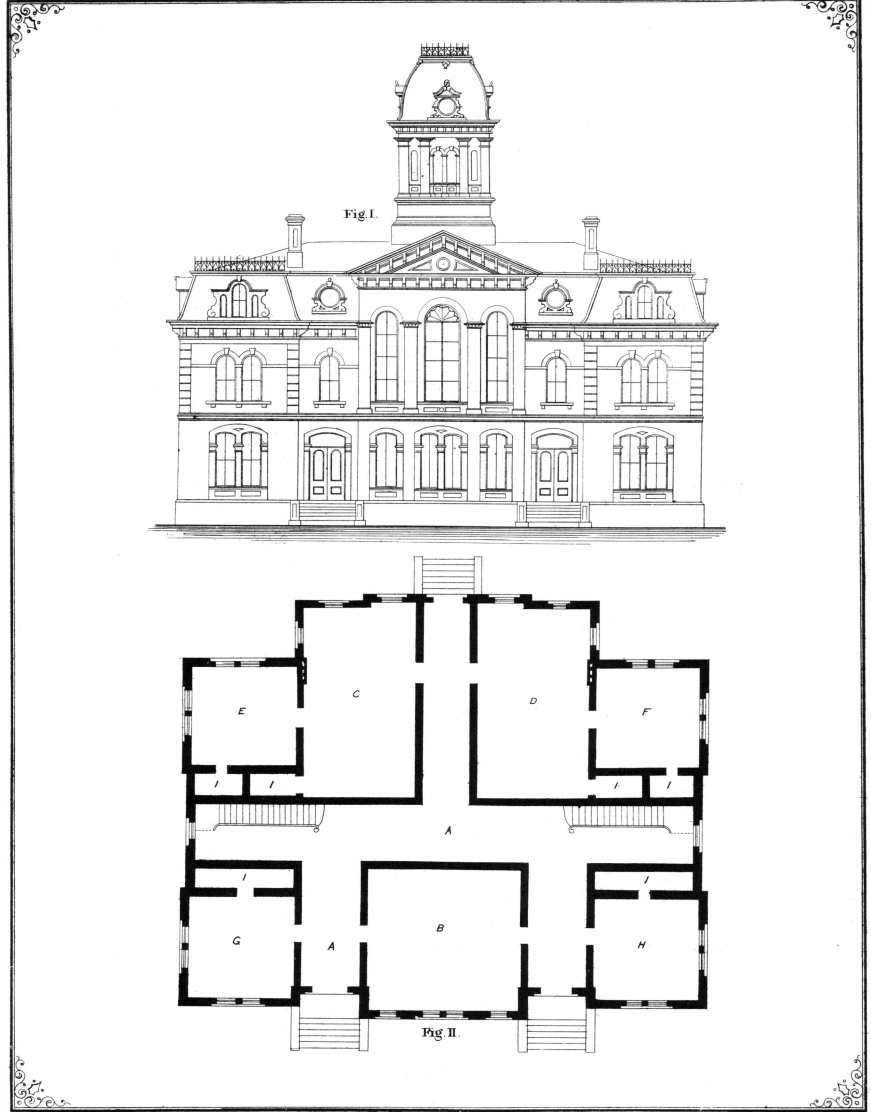

Fig. I.

Fig. II.

Lith by J.Bien 16 & 18 Park Place N.Y.

Plate 50.

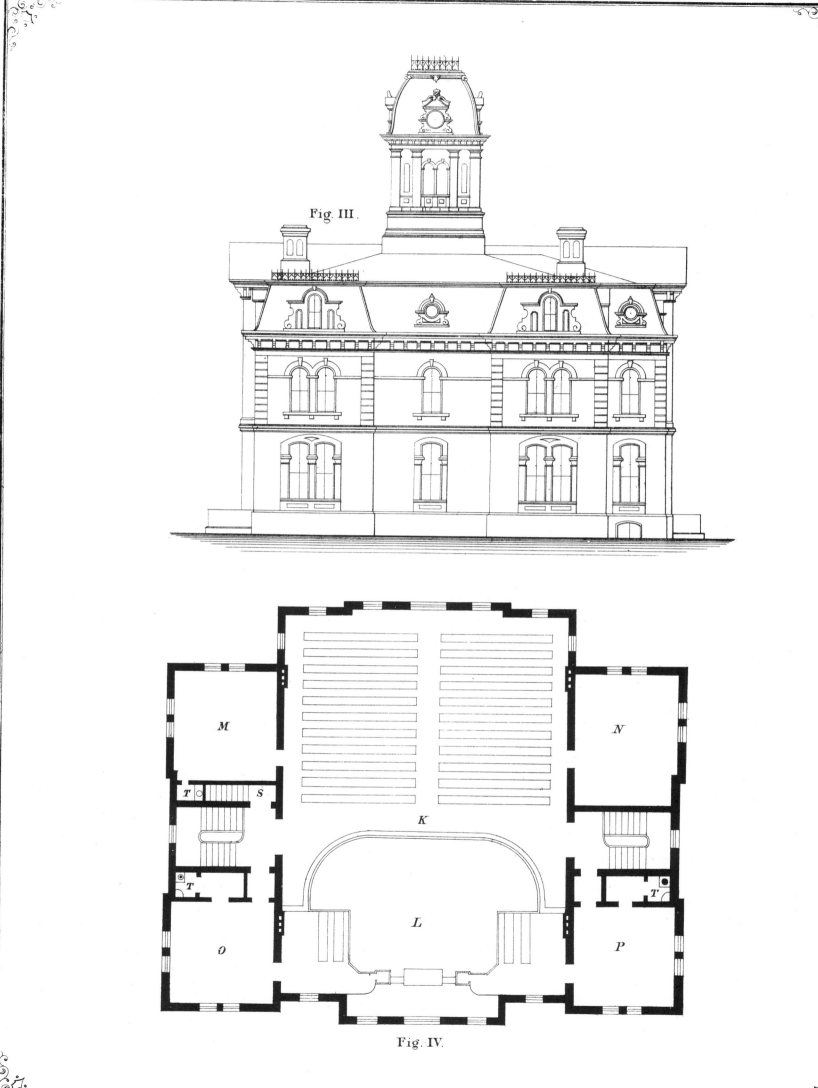

Fig. III.

Fig. IV.

Plate 51.

A

B

C

D

E

F

G

H

I

K

L

M

¼ full size.

N

¼ full size.

O

Scale ½ inch = 1 foot.

P

Q

R

½ inch = 1 foot.

Lith by J Bien 16 & 18 Park Place N.Y.

PLATES 52, 53, 54.

DESIGN FOR A MODEL JAIL AND JAILOR'S RESIDENCE.

E. E. MYERS, Architect, Springfield, Ill.

This design will be executed at Petersburg, Menard County, Ill., Similar jails have been erected at Carlinville, Macoupin County, and at Lincoln, Logan County, Ill. The foundation is stone. The superstructure of jailor's residence being brick, with stone dressings. The prison is dimension stone, all large size, pitch faced both sides twelve inches thick, and dowelled together with two-inch cannon shot, twelve shot to each stone. The cells, floors and ceilings are all six-inch slabs of stone. Complete cost, $20,000.

Plate 52. Front elevation, side elevation, basement ground plan, plan of first floor and plan of second floor. Scale, one-twelfth of one inch to the foot.

Plate 53. Longitudinal and transverse sections of building. Scale, one-eighth of one inch to the foot.

Plate 54. Design for outside and inside doors. Scale, one inch to the foot.

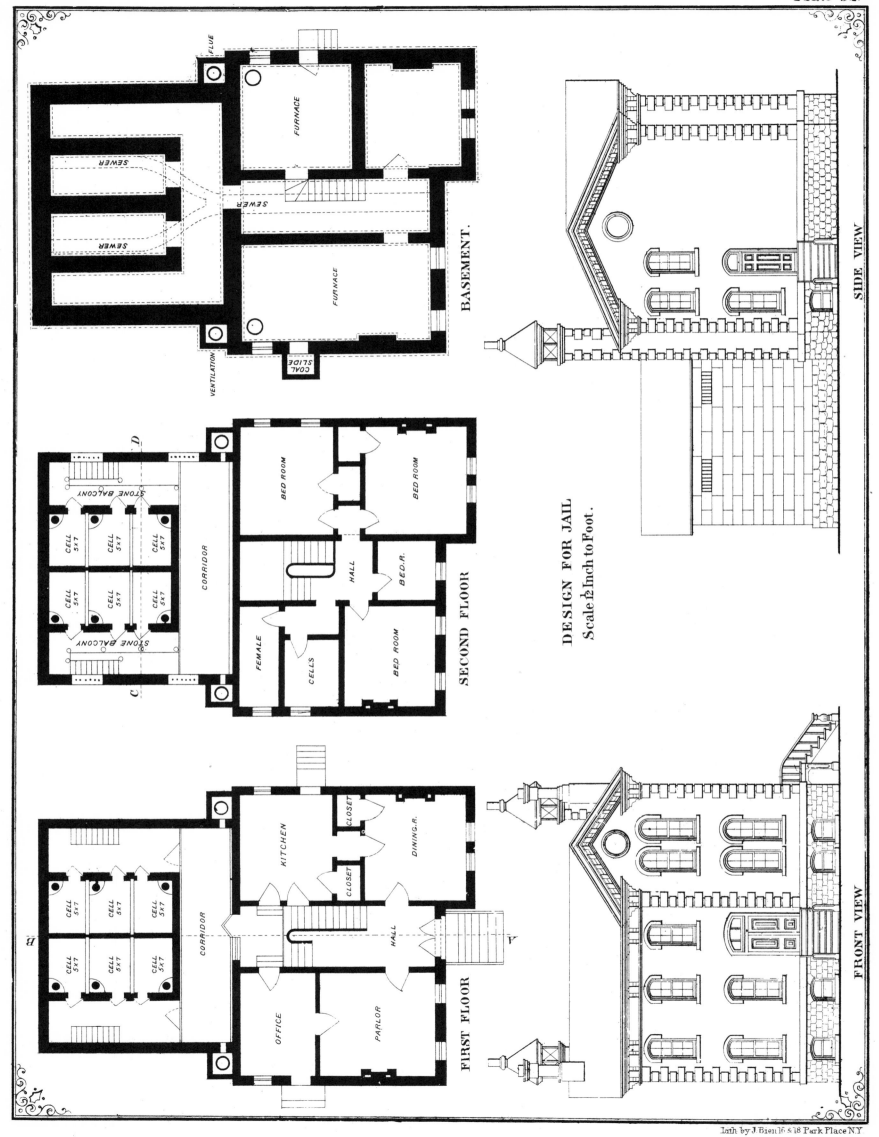

Plate 52.

BASEMENT.

FLUE

SEWER

SEWER

SEWER

FURNACE

FURNACE

VENTILATION

COAL SLIDE

SIDE VIEW

SECOND FLOOR

D

STONE BALCONY

CELL 5×7 CELL 5×7 CELL 5×7

CELL 5×7 CELL 5×7 CELL 5×7

CORRIDOR

STONE BALCONY

C

BED ROOM

BED ROOM

HALL

BED.R.

FEMALE

CELLS

BED ROOM

DESIGN FOR JAIL
Scale ½ Inch to Foot.

FIRST FLOOR

B

CELL 5×7 CELL 5×7 CELL 5×7

CELL 5×7 CELL 5×7 CELL 5×7

CORRIDOR

KITCHEN

CLOSET

CLOSET

DINING.R.

OFFICE

HALL

PARLOR

A

FRONT VIEW

Plate 53.

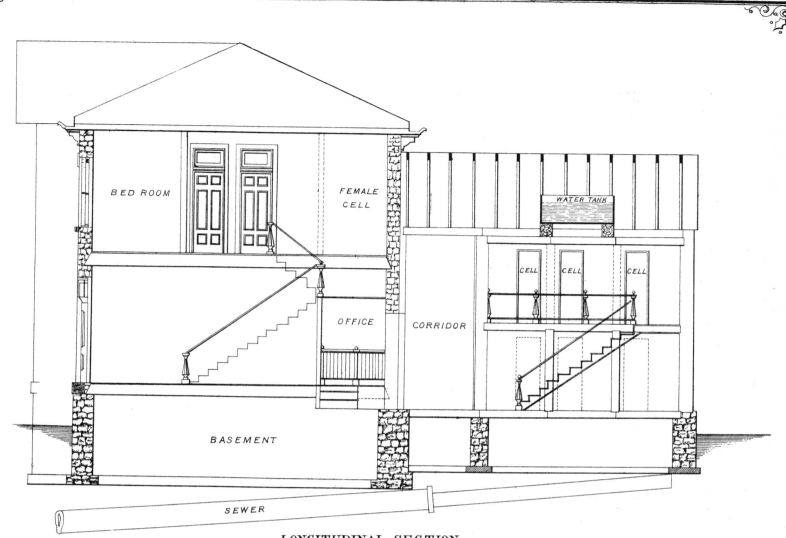

BED ROOM

FEMALE CELL

WATER TANK

CELL CELL CELL

OFFICE

CORRIDOR

BASEMENT

SEWER

LONGITUDINAL SECTION

Through A.B.

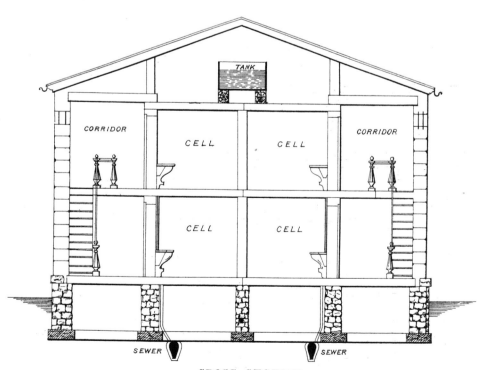

TANK

CORRIDOR

CELL CELL

CORRIDOR

CELL CELL

SEWER SEWER

CROSS SECTION

Through C.D.

Scale ⅜ inch to foot.

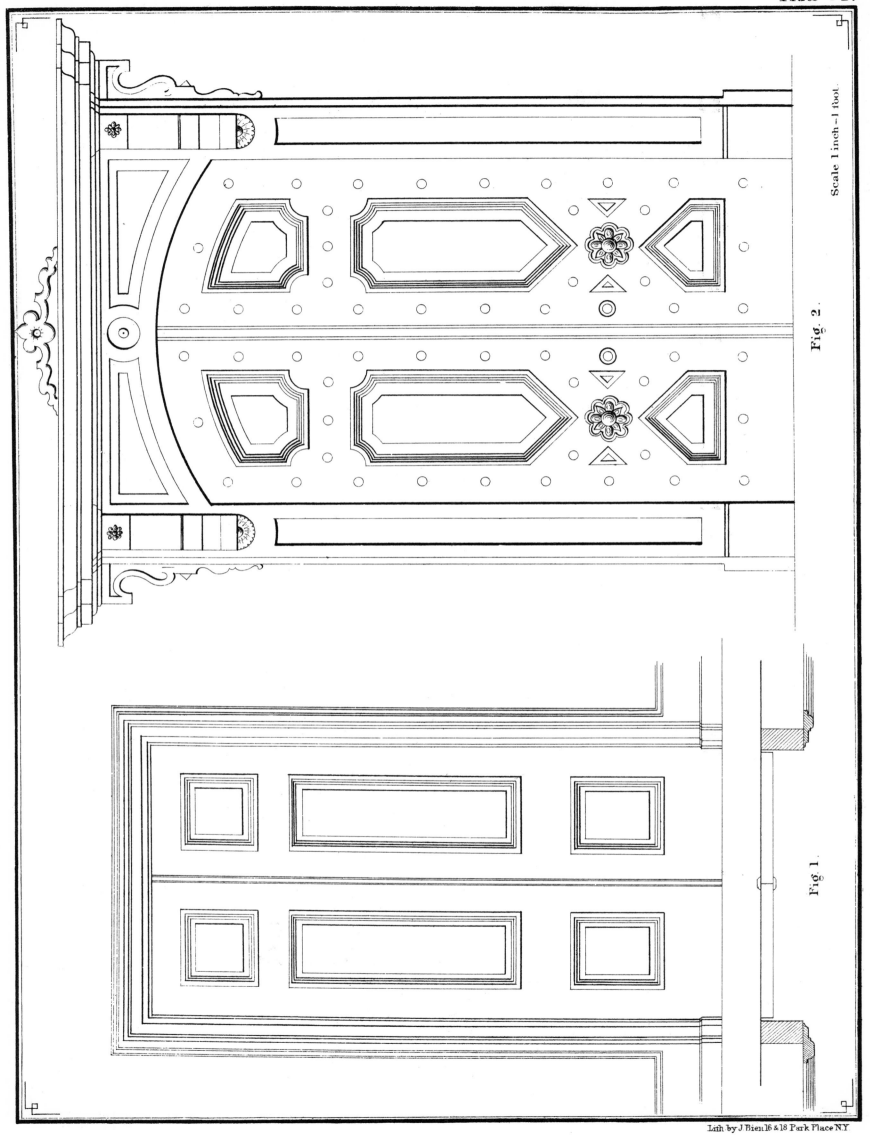

Plate 54.

Scale 1 inch = 1 foot.

Fig. 2.

Fig. 1.

Plate 55.

Inside finish for Stores, Banks and Insurance offices.

A

Scale ¾ in. to 1 foot.

C

D

E

Scale of B, C, D & E ½ in. to 1 foot.

B

SUPPLEMENT

TO

BICKNELL'S VILLAGE BUILDER,

CONTAINING

Eighteen Modern Designs

FOR

COUNTRY AND SUBURBAN HOUSES

OF MODERATE COST,

WITH

ELEVATIONS, PLANS, SECTIONS.

AND A VARIETY OF DETAILS, ALL DRAWN TO SCALE,

ALSO

A FULL SET OF SPECIFICATIONS, WITH APPROVED FORM OF CONTRACT, AND ESTIMATES OF COST.

———•———

New York:

A. J. BICKNELL & CO.,

ARCHITECTURAL BOOK PUBLISHERS,

27 WARREN STREET.

Architects who have Contributed to this Work.

———:o:———

D. B. Provoost, Elizabeth, N. J., Plates I., II., III., VI.
T. Thompson,   "   "   "   IV., XI., XII. & fig. 2 pl. XIII.
C. Graham & Son,   "   "   "   VII., VIII., IX., X., XV.
C. T. Rathbone, Pittsfield, Mass.,   "   XVI. and fig. 1 pl. XIII.
Lyman Underwood, Boston,   "   "   V.
B. H. Brooks,   "   "   "   XVIII., XIX.

Plate 2

Rafter, of deck

RAFTER

A

D

C

B

E

F

G

Side Elevation.
Scale ½ inch = one foot.

Plate 1. Front elevation, scale ¼ in. = 1 foot. Plate 2. Side elevation. Plate 3. Section and Plans.
A, Deck Cornice of main house. B, Dormer Window. C, Cornice of main house. D and E, Cornice, column and pedestal of piazza on main front. F, Window sill. G, Small bracket to main cornice. Scale, half-inch to one foot. Cost, with modern improvements, $5300.

Plate 3

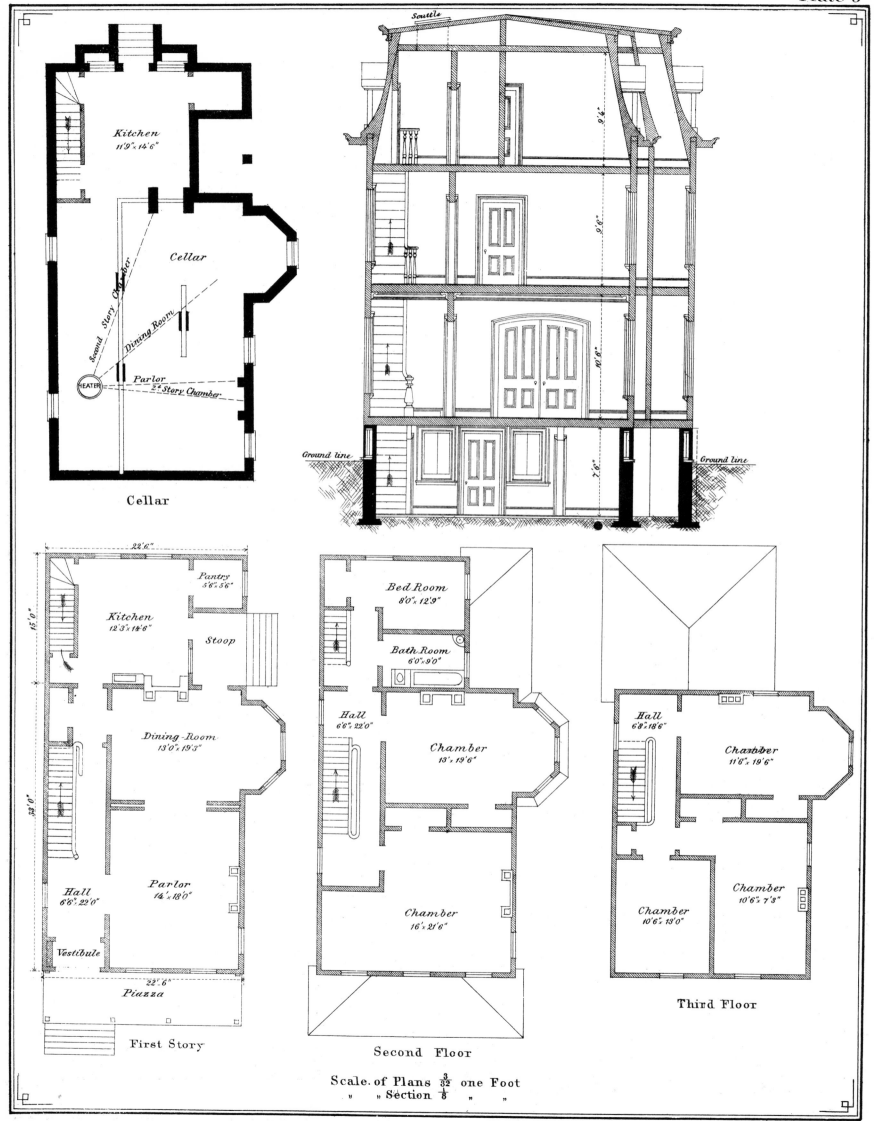

Kitchen
11'9" x 14'6"

Cellar

Second Story Chamber

Dining Room

Parlor

2nd Story Chamber

HEATER

Cellar

Scuttle

9'4"

9'6"

10'6"

7'6"

Ground line

Ground line

22'6"

Pantry
5'6" x 5'6"

15'0"

Kitchen
12'3" x 14'6"

Stoop

53'0"

Dining-Room
13'0" x 19'3"

Hall
6'6" x 22'0"

Parlor
14' x 18'0"

Vestibule

22'6"

Piazza

First Story

Bed Room
8'0" x 12'9"

Bath Room
6'0" x 9'0"

Hall
6'6" x 22'0"

Chamber
13' x 19'6"

Chamber
16' x 21'6"

Second Floor

Hall
6'8" x 18'6"

Chamber
11'6" x 19'6"

Chamber
10'6" x 7'3"

Chamber
10'6" x 13'0"

Third Floor

Scale of Plans $\frac{3}{32}$ one Foot
  „   „ Section $\frac{1}{8}$ „   „

DESIGN No. 1.

CARPENTER'S SPECIFICATION

Of work and materials used and required to build, erect and complete a two-story house, with basement and French roof, on lot No.   for   in accordance with plans and the within written specifications drawn and made by D. B. Provoost, Architect, Elizabeth, N. J.

DIMENSIONS.

For dimensions examine the plans and figures marked thereon.

HEIGHTS OF STORIES.

First Story,	-	-	10 ft. 6 in. clear of joist.	Third Story,	- - - 9 ft. 4 in. clear.
Second Story,	-	-	9 " 6 " main house.	Cellar,	- - - 7 " 6 "
" Story,	-	-	8 " 6 " kitchen ext.		

TIMBERS AND FRAMING.

Girder, 4x8 inches; Sills, 4x9 inches; Post Ties and Enterties, 4x6 inches; Plates, 4x5 inches; Hip and Valley Rafters, 2x8 and 2x7 inches; other Rafters, 2 x 6 inches, placed 2 feet from centers, first and second story floor-beams 2x9 inches. Third story floor beams 2x8 inches, all placed 16 inches, from centers, having two rows of truss bridging to each span, of 1½x3 inch spruce, tightly cut in and thoroughly nailed with tenpenny nails. Brace the building in the most thorough manner, with 3x4 joist, braced from sill to angle; outside studding around windows to be 3x4 joist; and fillng in timbers 2x4 inches, side rafters for French roof 1¼ inch thick spruce, placed 16 inches from centers; sills of piazza 3x6 inches, and filling in timbers 3x5, placed 5 feet from centers, with one length in center from sill to sill, plates 3x4 inch, rafters 3x4 inches, placed 2 feet from centers.

In the basement put down 5 inch faced chestnut post, placed 16 inches from centers, to lay the floor on, floor to be wide pine.

All the framing of the entire building to be done in the best manner, and all timbers to be free from shakes, splits, or dry rot, and the building to be raised straight, plumb, level and true ; all timbers to be spruce except floor beams, such to be hemlock.

ROUGH BOARDING.

Cover the entire frame with cull pine mill-worked boards, set at an angle of 45 degrees, and each length bracing to the opposite direction, and thoroughly nailed with tenpenny nails.

TARRED PAPER.

Cover the entire frame and roofs with a good quality tarred paper, stripped with masons' lath every 16 inches opposite the studding.

WINDOW FRAMES.

Build and set window frames as shown on the plans and elevation, with 2½ inch sills, except on rear, those 2 inches, with plank jambs, 1⅛ inch outside casings, moulded caps on front and sides, 1¾ inch sash on first story front, elsewhere 1½ inch sash, glazed with first quality French double thick sheet glass on first and second story main house, elsewhere single thickness; hang the sash with good axle pulls and strong hemp cord, fastened with the most approved sash fastenings; the two front windows on first story to have false heads in the frames, all to have cast iron weights; cellar windows to have sash with three lights wide, 1¼ sash, hung with 3 inch butts, and fasten open with a hook and staple, fastened to the floor beams, sash to be hung from the top.

CORNICE.

Build the cornice as shown on the elevation, with all its details fully and faithfully carried out on strong panel brackets, brackets to be on the sides and rear the same as shown on the front, and extension cornice to be in keeping with the house, but not as heavy as on main house; form good and capacious gutters and make them so as to drain dry.

FRENCH ROOF.

Slate the sides of the roof with slate 5x12 inches, cornered as shown on elevation, nailed with galvanized nails; all hips and valleys to be flushed with tin in the best manner.

TIN.

Cover the deck roof, roof of extension, piazzas, dormer, window caps, scuttle, gutters, flushing, &c., in the best manner, with the best brand of lead plate charcoal brand tin, all well locked, nailed and soldered and the whole work warranted water-tight; run the water to the ground through 3½ inch cross-tin leaders where shown and directed by owner.

PIAZZA.

Build and put up the piazzas as per plans and elevations, in the best manner, with all their details fully and faithfully carried out; lay the floors with narrow 1¼ inch pine flooring, laid in lead paint and neatly smoothed off and blind nailed, finished with a nosing and cone moulding. Build the steps of 1¼ inch pine, ⅞ risers, 1¼ inch opened strings, and steps finished in usual manner; cut work underneath facia to have a cut pattern and a base; build the columns of 5 inch solid pine, cornered to an octagon, with pedestals and cap, sheath underneath with narrow mill-worked pine boards beaded and blind nailed, finished in the angle with a cone moulding 1¼x1¼ inches.

SIDING.

Cover the entire sides and ends with clear narrow Michigan strips, laid not more than 4½ inches to the weather, all properly nailed, having the nail heads set in and all heading joints to be neatly smoothed off.

FLOORING.

Lay the floors of the first story with narrow 1 inch pine flooring, free from splits, shakes, large or loose knots, all blind nailed and neatly smoothed off. Second story and basement to be laid with 1¼ inch wide pine flooring. Third floor to be laid with 1 inch pine flooring, all thoroughly nailed with ten-penny nails.

PARTITIONS.

Set all the partitions where shown on the plans, with the main partitions, set with 3x4 joists, other partitions set with 2x4 wall strips, all to have the studs double at the doors, and set on a 3x4 joist top and bottom, put in a long brace of 3x4 inch joist wherever possible, and elsewhere put one row of bridging of 2x4 inch wall strips. Set all partitions straight, plumb and true, and thoroughly nailed. Do all blocking for cleats, bases, &c.

STAIRS.

Build the principal flight of stairs as shown on plans, from main to third story hall, of No. 1 pine, with 1¼ inch strings and treads, and 1 inch risers, the steps front and back tongued, return and mould the nosing of steps, and mould the string in a tasty manner; finish the wall string to correspond with the base in the hall, supported on two 3x6 inch timbers, bracketed to each tread, 8 inch fancy turned octagon newel, 4½x3 inch moulded hand-rail, and 1¾ inch fancy pattern balusters, newel, rail and balusters to be of seasoned black walnut, oiled two coats and made smooth at the final completion.

BACK STAIRS.

As shown on the plans, and built in the usual manner, neatly finished, having a newel, rail and balusters, of black walnut, such to be at the landing only. Stairs leading to basement to be a closed boxed string, 1¼ inch string and steps with ⅞ risers.

TRIMMINGS.

On the first story put plank jambs, open-faced architraves, 6 inches wide, returned $\frac{5}{8}$ bead, one member of moulding $1\frac{1}{4}x2\frac{1}{2}$ inches, $1\frac{1}{4}$ back band, wall member $\frac{7}{8}x1\frac{1}{2}$ inches, base 6 inches, one member of moulding (*besides the wall member*) $1\frac{3}{4}x2\frac{3}{4}$ inches, base scribed down to the floor; in hall, parlor and dining-room put down base blocks and panel backs, backs to have raised mouldings. Second floor, put plank jambs, 5 inch plain casings with returned $\frac{5}{8}$ bead, one member of moulding $1\frac{1}{4}x2\frac{1}{2}$ inches, back band $1\frac{1}{4}$ inches, scribed to the wall, or a small wall member, 6 inch base, scribed to the floor, and one member of moulding $1\frac{1}{4}x2\frac{1}{2}$ inches, such to be in the main house only; on the third floor, second story of extension, and in the basement, put down plank jambs, 5 inch plain casing and plain bead, with a $2\frac{1}{2}$ inch back-band moulding, 5 inch base, $\frac{7}{8}$ thick, and $1\frac{3}{4}$ inch moulding.

DOORS.

Hang all doors as follows: All passage doors hung with 4x4 wire jointed butts, closet doors hung with narrow 4 inch butts. All passage doors on first and second stories to have 5 inch mortise locks and porcelain furniture; on closets put reverse bevel 5 inch rim locks, same furniture; run the sliding doors between parlor and dining-room with 5 inch shives, run on a brass way let in the floor. Sliding doors to have ground glass in place of wood in the upper panels, 4 lights to each door. Vestibule and front doors to have English plate glass $\frac{1}{4}$ inch, doors made as per elevation, hung with 4x4 butts, acorn tips; fasten with flush bolts, 6 inch mortise locks and night latch attachment, and each lock to have two keys. In third story, kitchen extension and basement, put $4\frac{1}{2}$ inch rim locks, mineral furniture, except outside doors from basement, such to have 6 inch rim lock, and two sliding bolts, door to be 2 inches thick, hung with 4x4 butts, all doors to be No. 1 pine in four panels. Front vestibule and sliding doors to be 2 inches thick; all other passage doors to be $1\frac{1}{2}$ inches thick, and closet doors to be $1\frac{1}{4}$ inches thick.

BLINDS.

The octagon to have inside blinds made of pine, center sash made in four folds, and side sash three folds, hung with narrow butts and brass flaps, flaps to be from the inside, fastened with the most approved blind fastenings, and small porcelain knobs. Dormer windows to have inside blinds, made and finished as above, all other windows to have outside rolling blind shutters, hung and fastened in the most approved manner, painted three coats of pure lead color, to be chosen by the owner or agent.

BELLS.

Put up with copper wire in zinc tubes in a thorough workmanlike manner the gong and bells, the pulls to correspond in style and finish of their respective localities, one pull from front door to kitchen, one from dining-room, and one from the two front chambers on second story to kitchen, and one from chamber over dining room to servants' room.

BATH ROOM.

Fit up the Bath Room with walnut casing around bath-tub, water-closet and wash-basin, water-closet made plain, with a beaded case and cleated cover, hung with brass butts and screws, wash-stand to be made square, having panel sides, and small panel door in front, hung with brass butts and screws, and fastened with a small brass cupboard catch, bath-tub to have a paneled front, with small flush mouldings, same in panels of wash-stand, sheath the wall behind the bath-tub to the height of 3 feet from the top of tub, finished with a nosing cap and cove moulding.

CLOSETS.

All Closets to be shelved all around on three sides with $\frac{7}{8}$ inch beaded pine shelving, put up on rabbitted cleats, in the best manner, and all shelves to be left loose; all closets to have at an average of five shelves high, and an average of from 10 to 14 inches wide, all neatly smoothed off.

STATIONARY WASH TUBS.

Build and put up in the basement a set of three, Stationary Wash Tubs, made in the usual manner, sides, bottoms and ends to be $1\frac{1}{2}$ inches thick, of No. 1 pine, caps and lids $1\frac{1}{8}$ inches thick; clamp the lids and hang with narrow 3 inch butts, closed underneath with a $\frac{7}{8}$ pine board, the front left loose, clamped and fastened with two small iron buttons.

HEATER PIPES.

Heater Pipes of first quality cross tin, 8x8 inches, leading to first and second stories.

MISCELLANEOUS.

Put a Scuttle in the roof of main house, accessible from the hall, 2 ft. 6 by 3 feet, fasten down with 4 small hooks and staples ; build and provide a neat step-ladder made of ⅞ pine leading to roof.

Build a large Coal Bin in the cellar.

Put down black walnut saddles to all doors, with moulded edges.

Put down mitred borders to all hearth-stones.

Do all the work set forth on the drawings to their true extent and meanings, in case of any omission in this specification ; and all of the work to be done in a good and workmanlike manner ; all materials used not specified, to be good merchantable pine, and all materials mentioned, to be of the best of their several kinds.

PLUMBER'S SPECIFICATION.

Put in the bath-room a 12 oz. planished copper bath-tub 6 feet long, for both hot and cold water, having all the supply pipes, ⅝ inch, 2½ lbs. per foot, waste pipes, over-flows, &c., all complete.

WATER-CLOSET.

Put up one of Carr's Patent Monitor Closets, properly piped, having trap and screw ; connect lead waste-pipe to a 4 inch cast iron soil pipe ; soil pipe to be calked with lead and made water tight.

SINK.

Put up a cast-iron sink in the kitchen 18x36x6 inches, on cast-iron legs, supplied with both hot and cold water through ⅝ lead pipe, having over-flow, waste pipe, with trap and screw, &c., finished complete.

BOILER IN THE KITCHEN.

Put up a 40 gallon copper boiler, Brooklyn pressure, with all its connections properly made.

STATIONARY WASH TUBS.

To be supplied with hot and cold water through ¾ inch lead pipes, having over-flows, waste pipes, &c., all complete.

GAS.

Pipe the house for gas as follows : In the hall, parlor, dining-room, kitchen, and rooms over parlor and dining-room for drop-lights ; elsewhere in all rooms and halls put side-lights as, and where directed by owner, architect or agent.

RANGE.

Put in the kitchen a range to cost not less than seventy-five dollars, to be chosen by the owner.

MARBLE MANTLES.

Set in the parlor, dining-room and the rooms over the same, the cost of the four not to exceed three hundred dollars ; to be chosen by the owner.

Put up in the kitchen over the range a wooden mantle of a neat pattern.

PAINTER'S SPECIFICATION.

DIMENSIONS.

Examine the plans and figures marked thereon.

Paint the entire outside with three coats of Harrison Bros. & Co.'s "Town and Country" paints; color to be chosen by the owner; paint the tin work and chimneys with three coats of lead paint same as wood work.

GRAINING.

Grain the front and vestibule doors, and all doors and wood work on first story—all to be grained black walnut on two coats of lead paint; grain the kitchen in oak, on two coats of lead paint; grain the shutters to the octagon and dormer windows black walnut, as above mentioned; the newels, hand-rails and balisters are of black walnut, which are to be oiled and made smooth. All other inside wood-work to be painted three coats, as above mentioned. All to be done in a good workmanlike manner, and as soon as other work will permit.

MASON'S SPECIFICATION.

DIMENSIONS.

Examine the plans and figures marked thereon.

EXCAVATION AND FOUNDATION.

Excavate the building to the depth and form marked on the plans. Starting the foundation 6 inches below the cellar floor on a good base course made with brick, and run the walls up to the ground line 12 inches thick, and from there up 8 inches thick; build the piers as shown on plans 12x24 inches, the piers for the chimneys properly bound together, using no bats except for closers, laid with close joints, and with good lime and sand mortar. All to be good North River brick and stone lime.

LATH, PLASTERING, &c.

Lath, scratch coat, brown, and hard-finish the entire building.

CHIMNEYS.

Build the chimneys as per plans, and properly core the same, putting in heater pipes, as and where shown in heater specification, the chimneys to be built of pale North River brick, turn arches over fire places and under hearth-stones.

CORNICES.

Put up in parlor and dining-room a neat, plain cornice 7 inches on the wall and 9½ on the ceiling; in hall and rooms on second-story over parlor and dining-room, run a cornice 6 inches on the wall, and 8 on the ceiling.

CENTERPIECES.

Put up centerpiece in parlor, dining-room, hall, and the two rooms above; the whole not to cost less than thirty-six dollars.

FINALLY

Concrete the cellar floor; cement the foundation from the outside, and lay off in blocks. Put 3-inch flag-stone sills to all cellar windows.

Build areas around windows in rear, the steps leading to the basement to have 3-inch flag-stone steps and brick risers. Build piers for the piazza columns 12-inches square, set 2 feet below the ground.

All the work to be done in a good workmanlike manner.

APPROVED FORM OF CONTRACT.

Articles of Agreement, made the

day of   One Thousand Eight Hundred and

Seventy   **Between**

of the First Part, and

of the Second Part

The part   of the second part, in consideration of the covenants and agreements hereinafter contained to be kept and performed by the part   of the first part, and of One Dollar, the receipt whereof the part   of the second part hereby acknowledge, do   covenant, promise and agree, to and with the part   of the first part, that   the part   of the second part, will erect, build and complete or cause to be erected, built and completed, on the land of the part   of the first part

good and substantial building   to wit:

of the dimensions, description and materials, mentioned and specified in the written paper entitled "Specification of the   work and materials," signed by said parties, and bearing even date herewith, and according to a plan made by

with reference to which said specification is drawn; and will provide at   own expense all the materials necessary for the erecting and completing said building   according to said plan and specification; and will deliver said building   to the part   of the first part completely finished, and ready for the occupation of tenants, on the

unless such delivery be prevented by accidental fire or by circumstances over which the said part   of the second has or could have no control.

The part   of the first part, in consideration of the covenants and agreements aforesaid to be kept and performed by the part   of the second part, do   covenant, promise and agree, to and with the part   of the second part, the said part   of the second part performing the covenants and agreements on   part,   the part   of the first part will pay or cause to be paid, unto the part of the second part, for erecting and completing said building   in manner aforesaid, and providing the materials therefor, the sum of   Dollars, lawful money of the United States of America, to be paid in the following manner:

Provided That in each of the said cases a certificate shall be obtained, signed by the said Architect or Superintendent.

And it is hereby mutually Covenanted and Agreed, between the said parties, that the part of the first part may make, or require to be made, alterations in the plan of construction from that herein and in said specification and plan expressed, without annulling or invalidating this agreement; and that, in case of any such alterations, the increase or diminution of expense occassoned thereby shall be estimated according to the price fixed by these presents for the whole work and materials, and allowance shall be made on one side or the other, as the case may be. **And** that if there shall be any delay on the part of the part of the second part, in erecting or completing said building that in the opinion of the superintendent will prevent being completed on the day herein specified, then the part of the first part may, after three days' notice, in writing, being given, at option, either employ persons other than the part of the second part to do the whole or any part of said work, and furnish the whole or any part of said materials, and deduct the cost of the same from the sum hereinbefore agreed to be paid by the part of the first part, or leave the completion of said building unto the part of the second part, and enforce claim for damages should said building be not completed on the day herein specified. **And** it is further agreed, that if the said building shall not be finished and completed in manner aforesaid, by the said

the said part of the second part shall forfeit the sum of

Dollars,

for each and every day from and after that time during which the said building shall remain unfinished and not completed as aforesaid, to be deducted from the sum herein before agreed to be paid by the part of the first part. **And that** in case of any disagreement between said parties, relating to the performance of any covenant or agreement

herein contained, such disagreement shall be referred to three disinterested persons, (one to be chosen on each side, and they two to choose another,) the decision in writing, signed by any two of whom, shall be final. **And** for the true performance of the said covenants and agreements on their part respectively, the said parties bind themselves, to part of the first part to the part of the second part, and the part of the second part to the part of the first part, their heirs, executors and assigns, firmly by these presents, in the penal sum of

Dollars.

In Witness Whereo., the said parties have hereunto set their hands and seals, the day and year first above written.

Sealed and Delivered ⎫
in the presence of ⎰

Plate 4

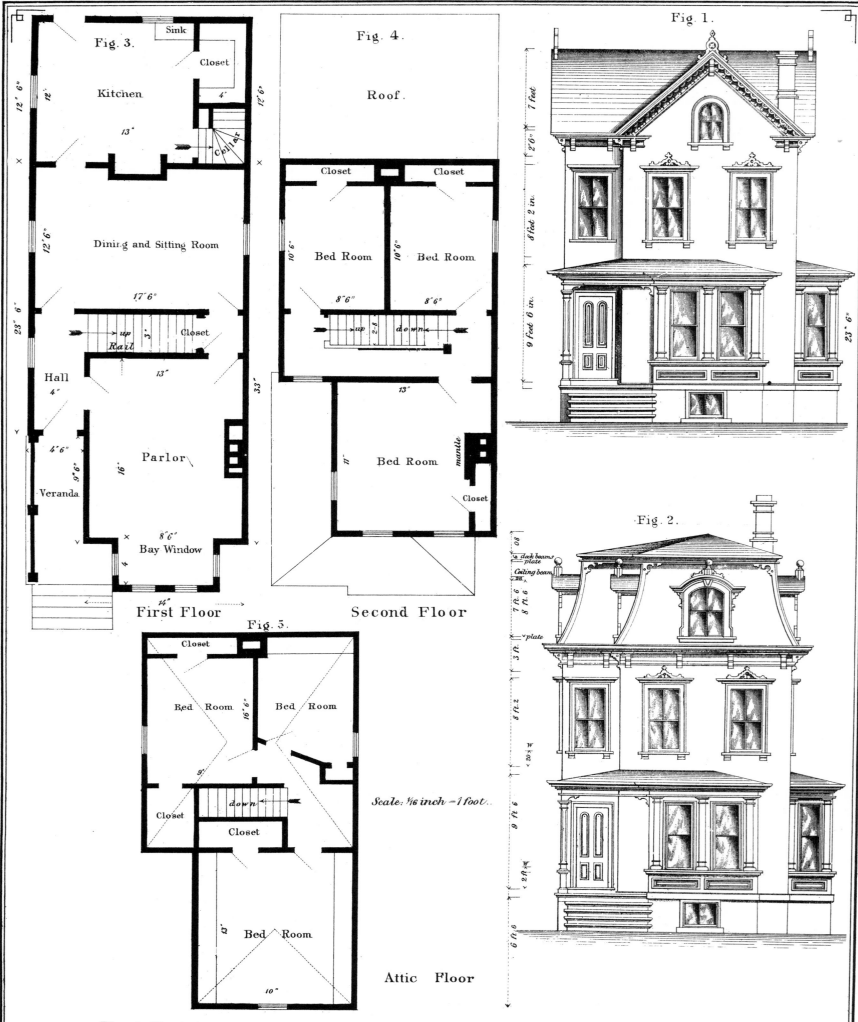

Fig. 1.

Fig. 3.

Sink

Closet

Kitchen

Cellar

Dining and Sitting Room

17' 6"

up
Rail
3'
Closet

13"

Hall
4"

4' 6"

Parlor

16'

9' 6"

Veranda

8' 6"
Bay Window

14'

First Floor

Fig. 4.

Roof.

Closet   Closet

Bed Room   Bed Room

8' 6"   8' 6"

up   down

13"

Bed Room

mantle

Closet

Second Floor

Fig. 5.

Closet

Bed Room   Bed Room

16' 6"

9'

Closet

down

Closet

Bed Room

10"

Attic Floor

Scale: 1/16 inch = 1 foot.

Fig. 2.

Fig. 1. Erected with a balloon-frame well braced, studding outside covered with thick cane fibre paper, clapboarded, main roof shingled, rear wing metal roof, plain trimmings inside, hard wall first and second floors, one coat white-wash wall in attic, neat cornice in parlor and dining-room, with marble mantels first floor.   Cost, $2500.

Fig. 2. Finished same as Fig. 1.   The bay windows were intended for the dining-room, but were not used in the execution of the designs, therefore are not shown on the plans.   Cost, $3200.

Plate 5

Front Elevation

9' 0"

10' 0"

ENTRY PANTRY CHINA CLOSET

KITCHEN DINING ROOM

DOWN

UP

HALL

PARLOR

Plan of First Floor

CHAMBER CHAMBER

CLOSET

DOWN

HALL CLOSET CLOSET

CLOSET

BED ROOM CHAMBER

Plan of Second Floor.

Scale: 8 feet to 1 inch.
Cost $. 3500.

Plate 6

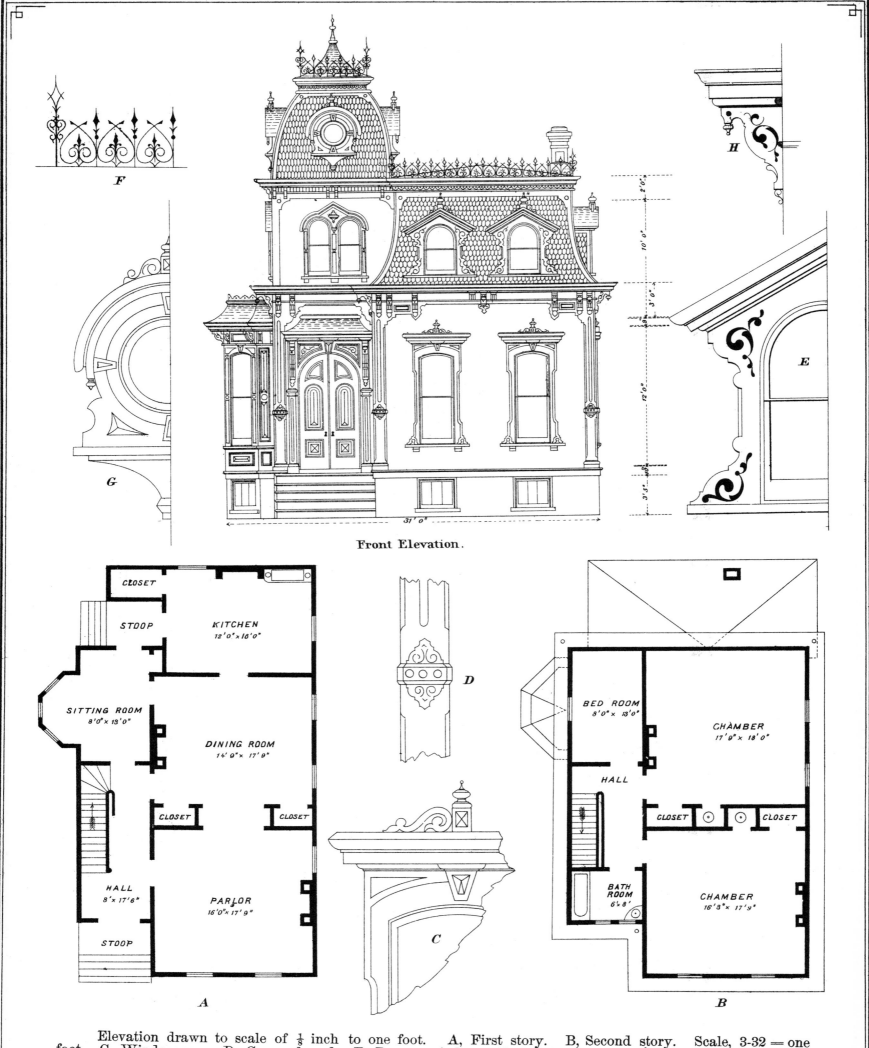

Front Elevation.

F

H

G

E

CLOSET

STOOP

KITCHEN
12'0" x 16'0"

SITTING ROOM
8'0" x 13'0"

DINING ROOM
14'9" x 17'9"

D

CLOSET   CLOSET

HALL
8' x 17'6"

PARLOR
16'0" x 17'9"

STOOP

C

A

BED ROOM
8'0" x 13'0"

CHAMBER
17'9" x 18'0"

HALL

CLOSET   CLOSET

BATH
ROOM
6'x 8'

CHAMBER
16'3" x 17'9"

B

Elevation drawn to scale of ⅛ inch to one foot. A, First story. B, Second story. Scale, 3-32 = one foot. C, Window cap. D, Corner board. E, Dormer window. F, Cresting on main roof and tower. G, Dormer on tower. H, Cornice and bracket on main cornice. Details to scale of ½ inch to one foot. Cost, with improvements, $4200.

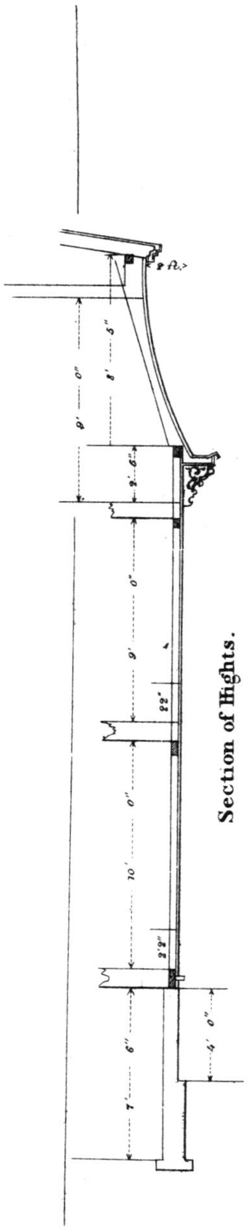

Plate 7

Section of Hights.

Front Elevation.

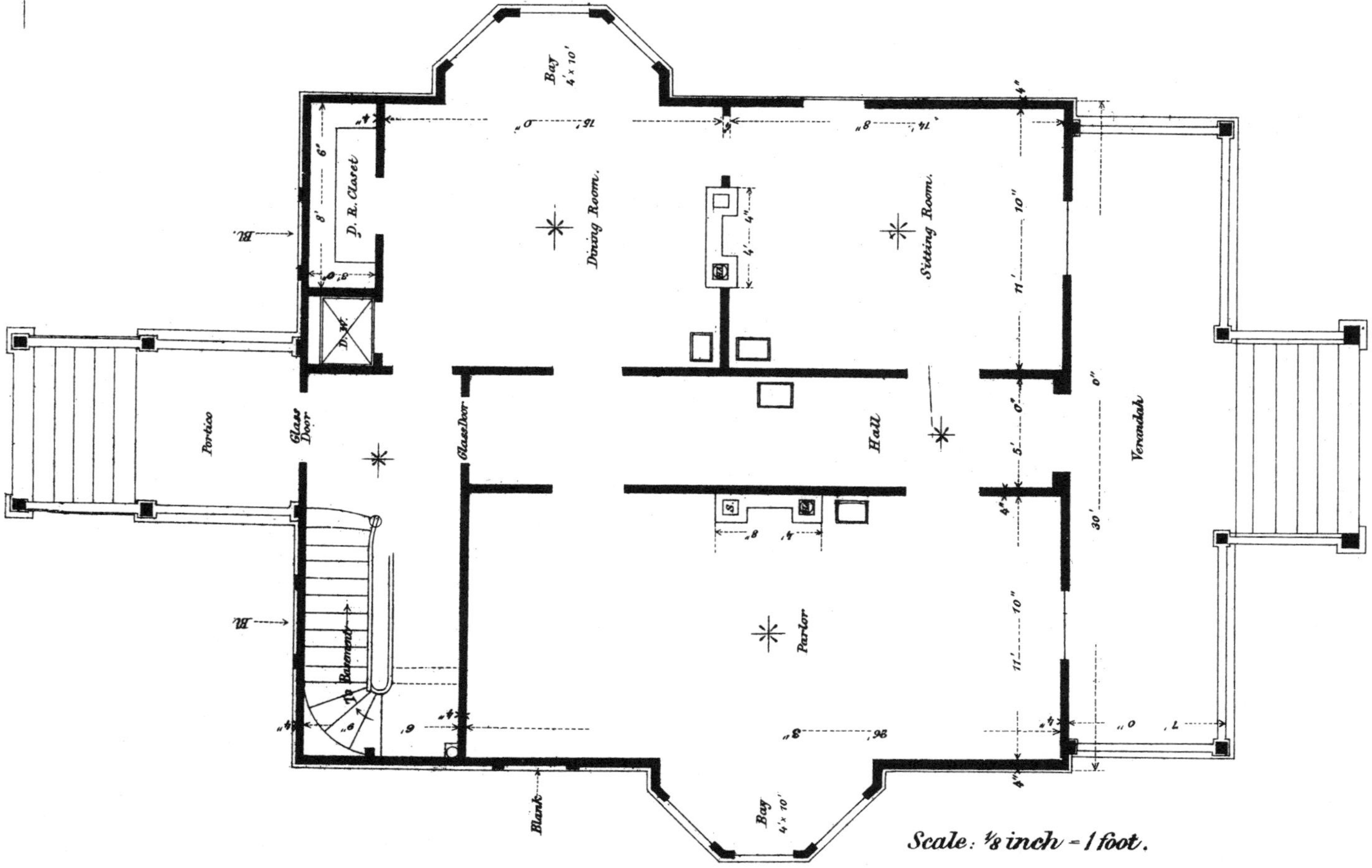

First Floor.

Bay 4' x 10'

D. R. Closet.

Draing Room.

Sitting Room.

Portico

Glass Door

Glass Door

Hall

Verandah

Parlor

Bay 4' x 10'

Scale: ⅛ inch = 1 foot.

Plate 8

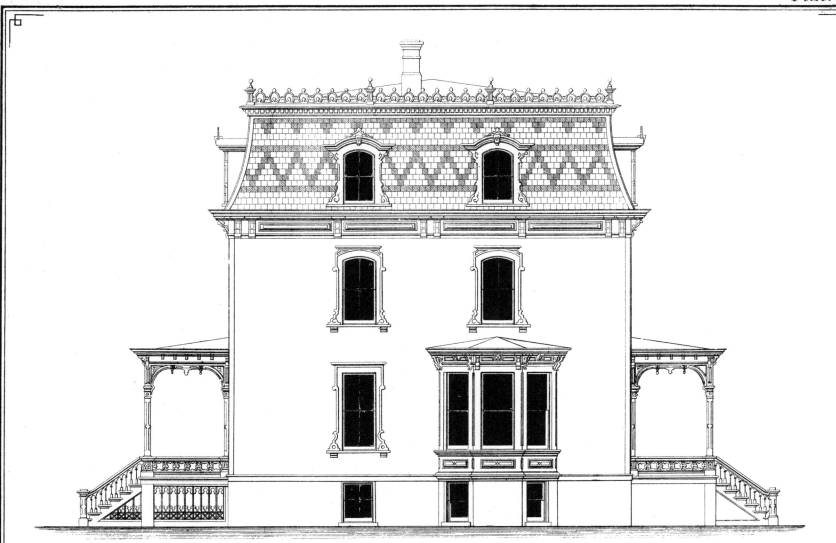

Side Elevation.
Scale: ⅛ inch = 1 foot.

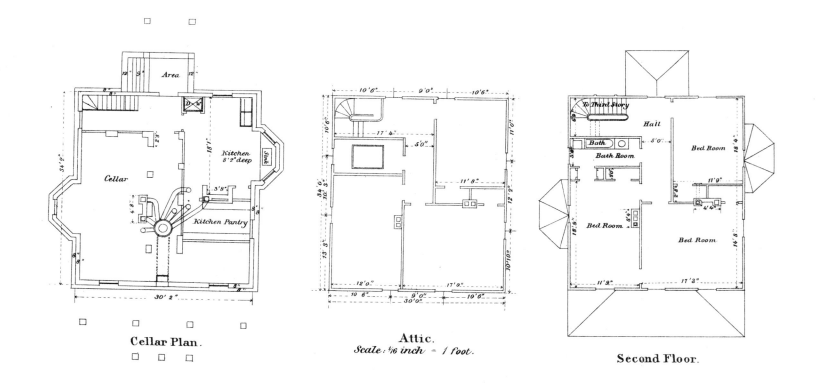

Cellar Plan.

Attic.
Scale: ⅙ inch = 1 foot.

Second Floor.

Plates 7 and 8, Front and Side Elevations and Plans of a square French roof dwelling, giving a very liberal arrangement at a cost from $5500 to $7000, owing to locality and style of finish.

Plate 9

4˝ Rise

4˝ Rise

8' 0˝

9' 0˝

10' 6˝

Front Elevation
Scale: 1 inch = 4 feet.

Plate 10

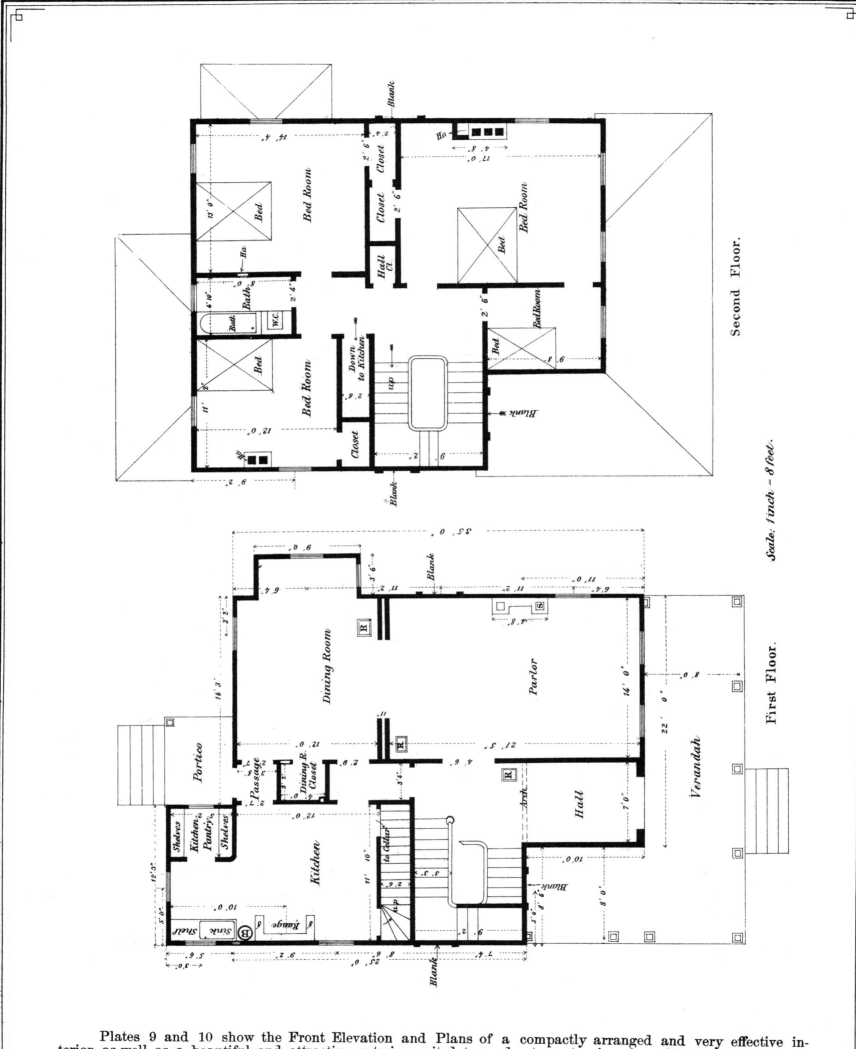

Second Floor.

Scale: 1 inch = 8 feet.

First Floor.

Plates 9 and 10 show the Front Elevation and Plans of a compactly arranged and very effective interior, as well as a beautiful and attractive exterior, suited to moderate cost; viz.: from $5000 to $7000, owing to locality.

Plate 11

Scale: 4 feet to 1 inch.

Plate 12

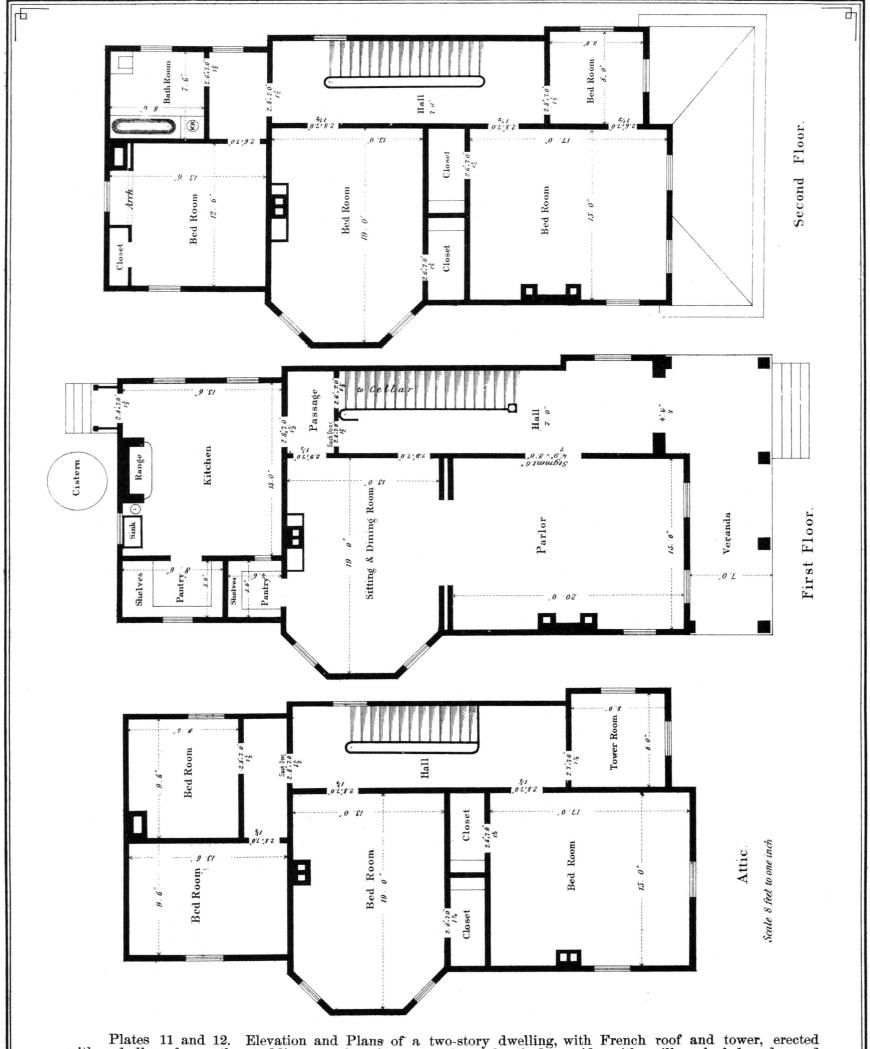

Second Floor.

Bath Room 7.6"

Bed Room 8.0"

Bed Room 12.6"

Arch

Closet

Hall 7.0"

Closet

Closet

Bed Room 19.0"

Bed Room 15.0"

First Floor.

Cistern

Range

Sink

Kitchen 15.0"

Shelves

Pantry 5.0"

Shelves

Pantry 5.0"

Passage

to Cellar

Sash Door

Hall 7.0"

Sitting & Dining Room 19.0"

Segment.

Parlor 15.0"

Veranda 7.0"

20.0"

Attic.

Scale 8 feet to one inch

Bed Room 7.6"

Tower Room 8.0"

Bed Room 9.6"

Bed Room 9.6"

Hall 7.0"

Closet

Closet

Bed Room 19.0"

Bed Room 15.0"

Plates 11 and 12. Elevation and Plans of a two-story dwelling, with French roof and tower, erected with a balloon-frame, the studding one length up to plate, sheathed outside with mill-worked boards, and painted two coats outside and inside; marble mantels, both stories; 8-inch foundation walls; hard wall on two coats of brown wall, first and second stories; one coat brown wall and hard wall on attic; parlor, hall and dining-room corniced and neat centres first story. Complete cost, $5000. to **$6000.**

Plate 13

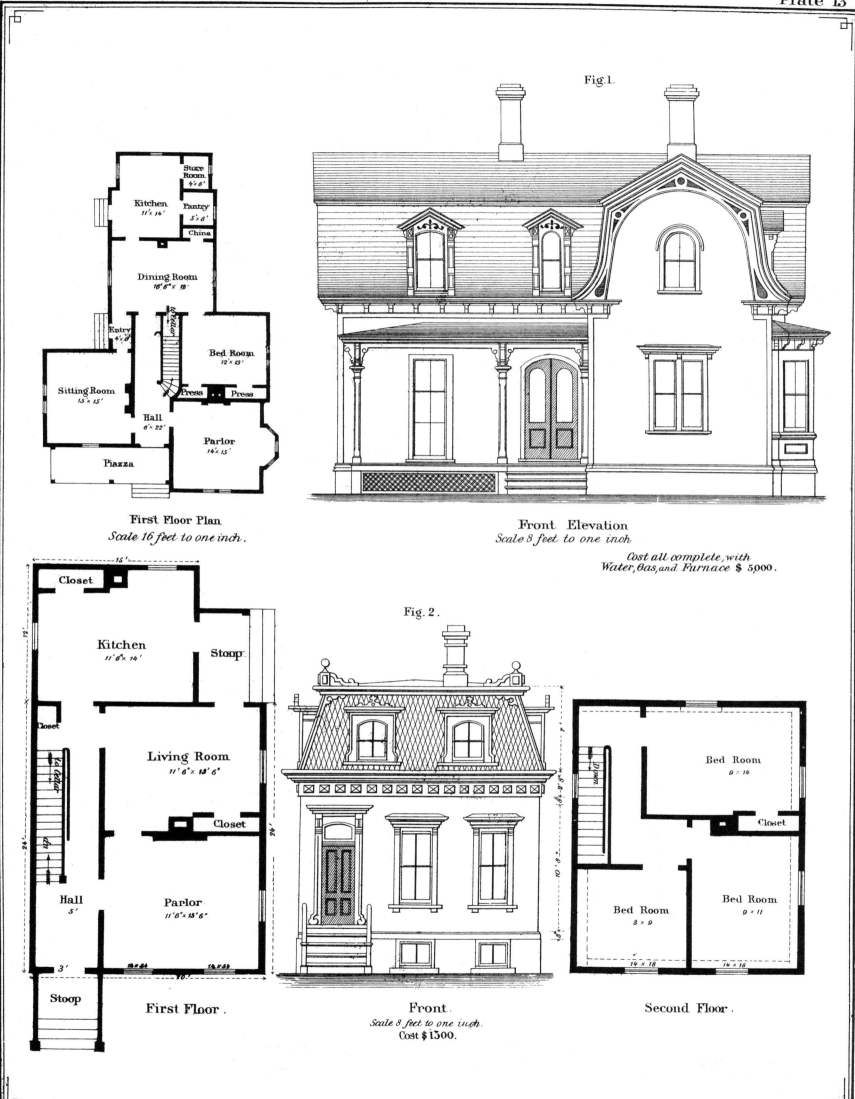

Fig.1.

First Floor Plan
Scale 16 feet to one inch.

Store Room 4'x 6'
Kitchen 11'x 14'
Pantry 5'x 6'
China
Dining Room 16' 6"x 18'
Entry 4'x 6'
Bed Room 12'x 13'
Sitting Room 15'x 15'
Press   Press
Hall 6'x 22'
Parlor 14'x 15'
Piazza

Front Elevation
Scale 8 feet to one inch.

*Cost all complete, with
Water, Gas, and Furnace $ 5,000.*

Fig. 2.

Closet
Kitchen 11'6"x 14'
Stoop
Closet
Living Room 11'6"x 13'6"
Closet
Hall 5'
Parlor 11'6"x 13'6"
Stoop

First Floor.

Front.
Scale 8 feet to one inch.
Cost $1300.

Bed Room 9 x 14
Down
Closet
Bed Room 8 x 9
Bed Room 9 x 11

Second Floor.

Plate 14.

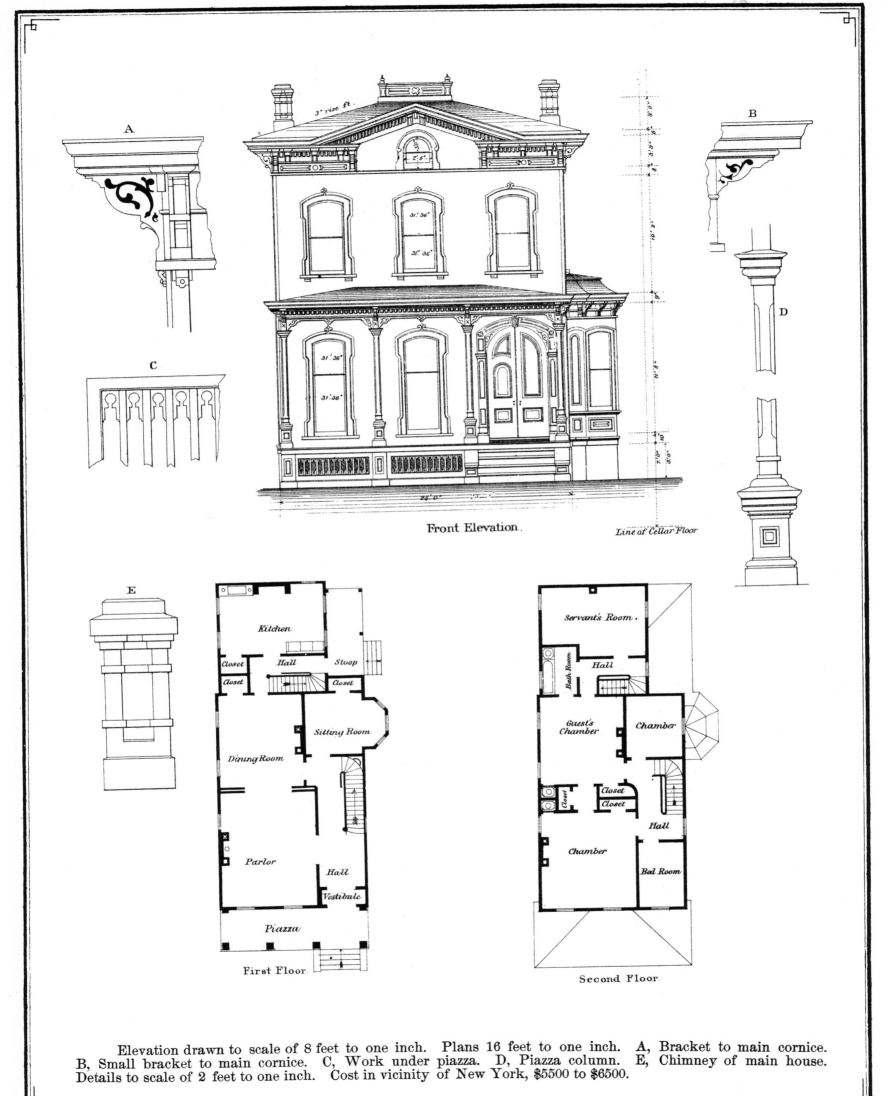

A

B

C

D

E

3" rise ft.

2' 6"

3'. 36"

3'. 36"

3'. 36"

3'. 36"

25' 0"

Front Elevation.

Line of Cellar Floor

First Floor plan:
Kitchen
Closet
Closet
Hall
Stoop
Closet
Sitting Room
Dining Room
Parlor
Hall
Vestibule
Piazza

First Floor.

Second Floor plan:
Servant's Room.
Bath Room
Hall
Guest's Chamber
Chamber
Closet
Closet
Closet
Hall
Chamber
Bed Room

Second Floor.

Elevation drawn to scale of 8 feet to one inch.   Plans 16 feet to one inch.   A, Bracket to main cornice.
B, Small bracket to main cornice.   C, Work under piazza.   D, Piazza column.   E, Chimney of main house.
Details to scale of 2 feet to one inch.   Cost in vicinity of New York, $5500 to $6500.

Plate 15

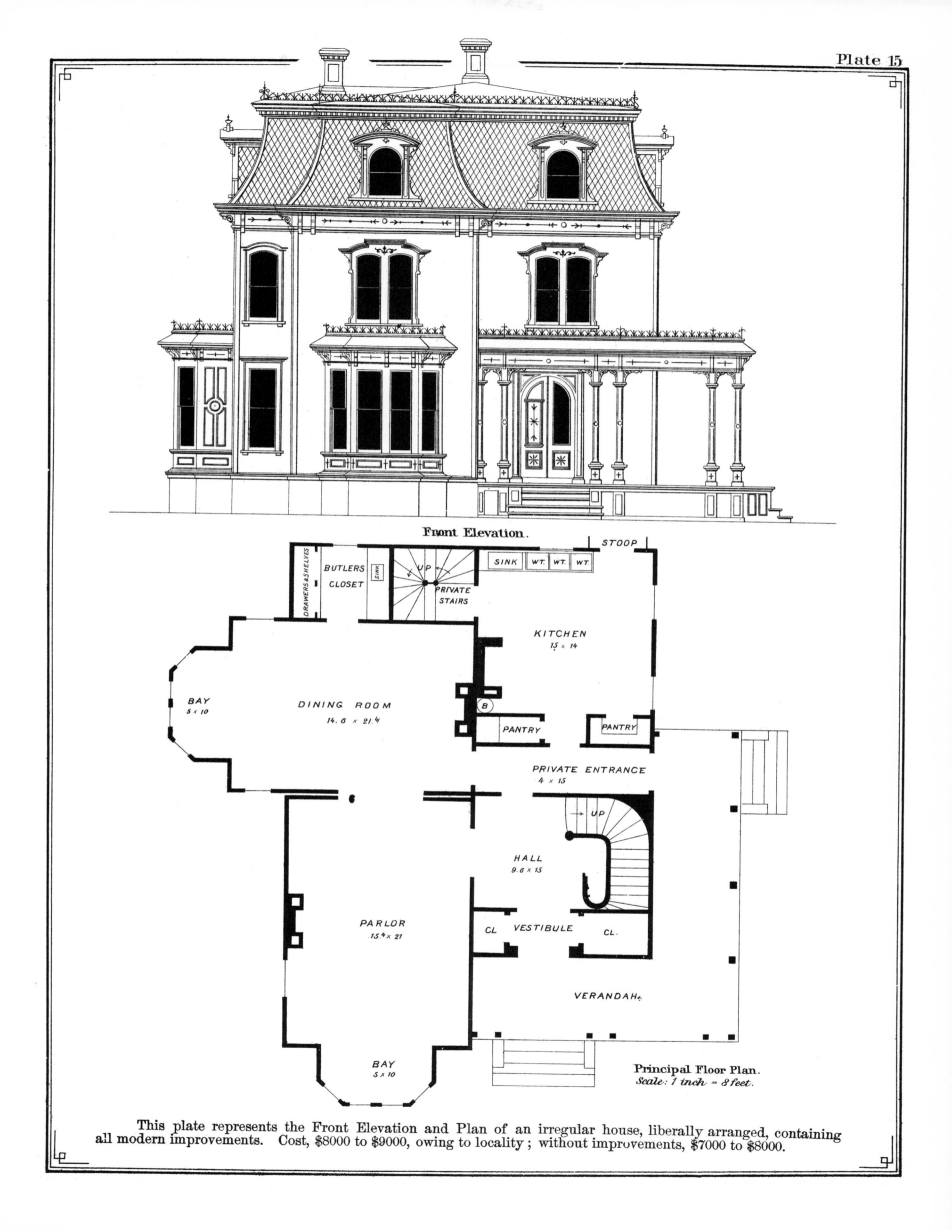

Front Elevation.

STOOP

DRAWERS&SHELVES

BUTLERS CLOSET

SINK

UP

PRIVATE STAIRS

SINK | WT. | WT. | WT.

KITCHEN
15 x 14

BAY
5 x 10

DINING ROOM
14. 6 x 21.4

B

PANTRY

PANTRY

PRIVATE ENTRANCE
4 x 15

UP

HALL
9.6 x 15

PARLOR
15.4 x 21

CL

VESTIBULE

CL.

VERANDAH.

BAY
5 x 10

Principal Floor Plan.
Scale: 1 inch = 8 feet.

This plate represents the Front Elevation and Plan of an irregular house, liberally arranged, containing all modern improvements.   Cost, $8000 to $9000, owing to locality ; without improvements, $7000 to $8000.

Plate 16

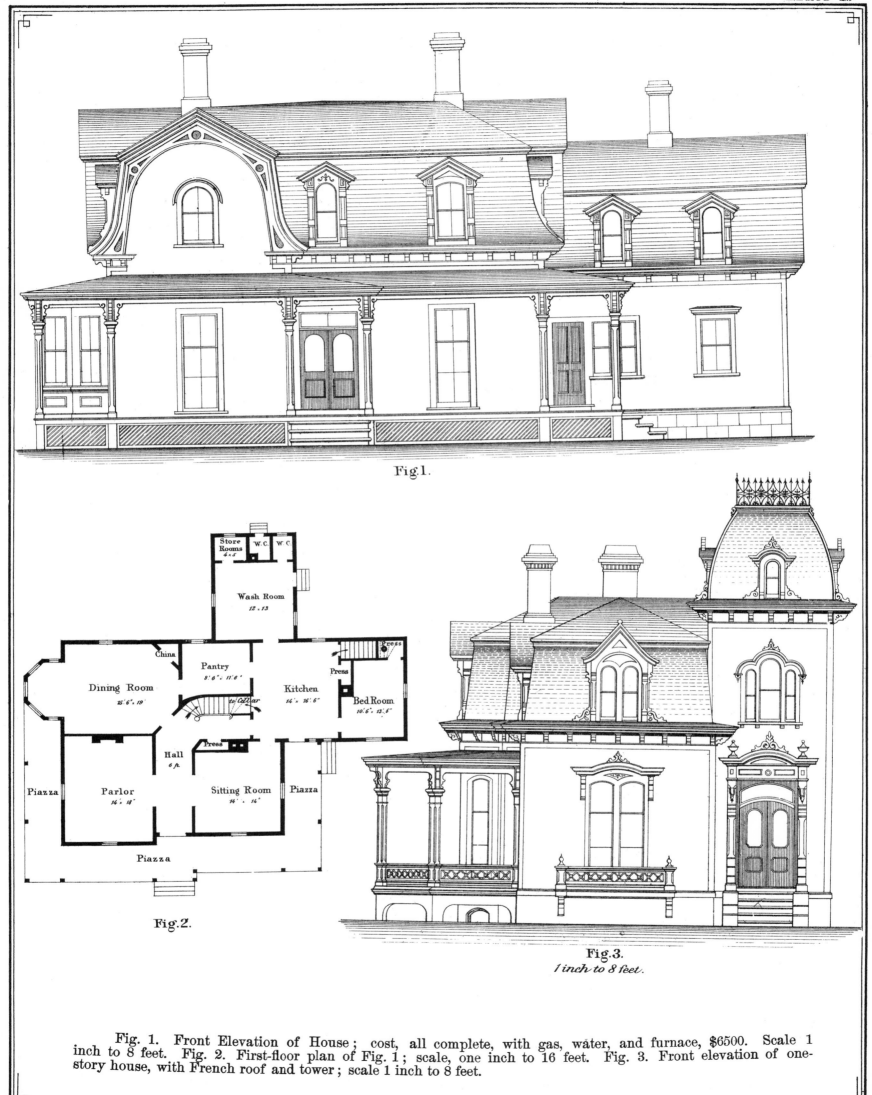

Fig. 1.

Fig. 2.

Fig. 3.
1 inch to 8 feet.

Fig. 1. Front Elevation of House; cost, all complete, with gas, water, and furnace, $6500. Scale 1 inch to 8 feet. Fig. 2. First-floor plan of Fig. 1; scale, one inch to 16 feet. Fig. 3. Front elevation of one-story house, with French roof and tower; scale 1 inch to 8 feet.

Plate 17

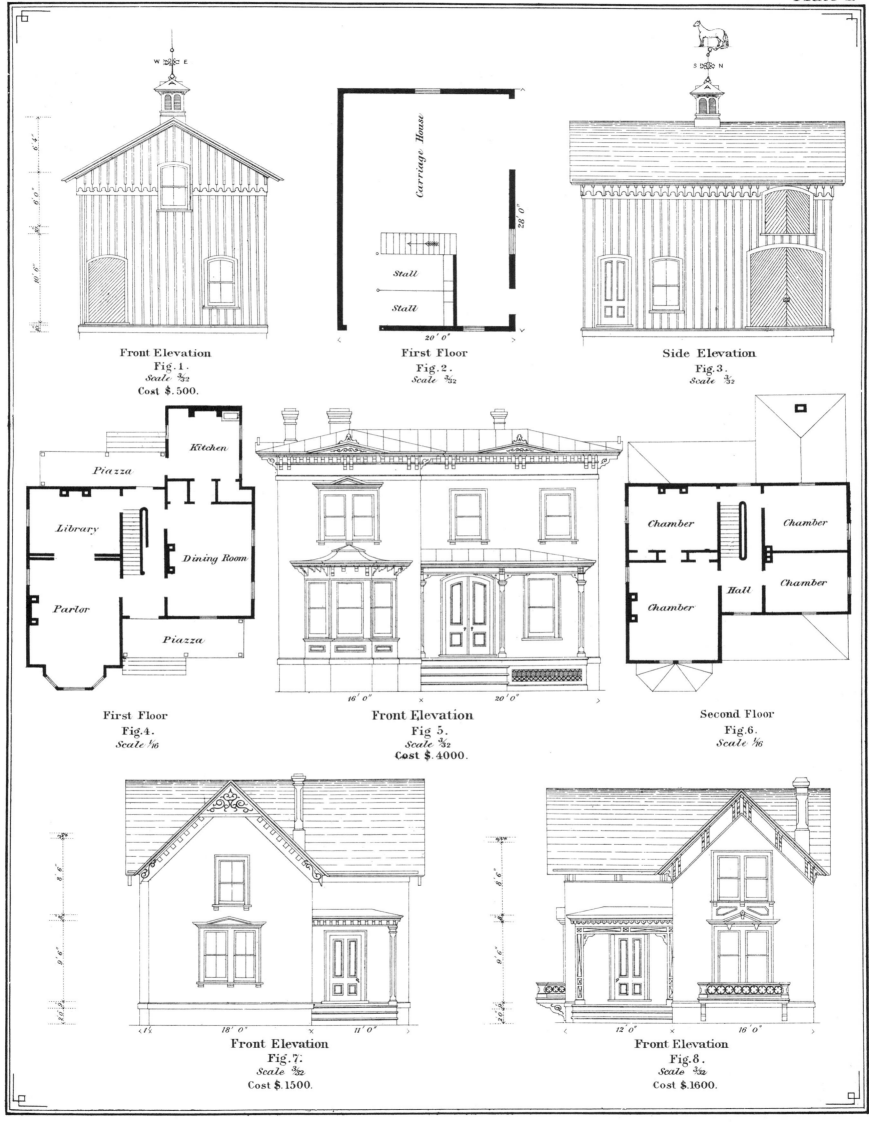

Front Elevation
Fig. 1.
Scale 3/32
Cost $. 500.

First Floor
Fig. 2.
Scale 3/32

Side Elevation
Fig. 3.
Scale 3/32

Carriage House

Stall

Stall

First Floor
Fig. 4.
Scale 1/16

Front Elevation
Fig 5.
Scale 3/32
Cost $. 4000.

Second Floor
Fig. 6.
Scale 1/16

Kitchen

Piazza

Library

Dining Room

Parlor

Piazza

Chamber

Chamber

Chamber

Hall

Chamber

Front Elevation
Fig. 7.
Scale 3/32
Cost $. 1500.

Front Elevation
Fig. 8.
Scale 3/32
Cost $. 1600.

Plate 18

Front Elevation

Scale 8 ft. to 1 inch.

Plan of First Floor

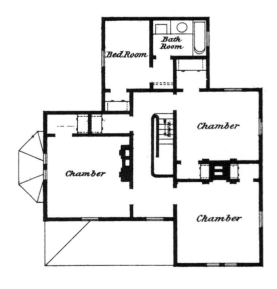

Plan of Second Floor

Scale 16 ft. to 1 inch.
Cost $.3300.

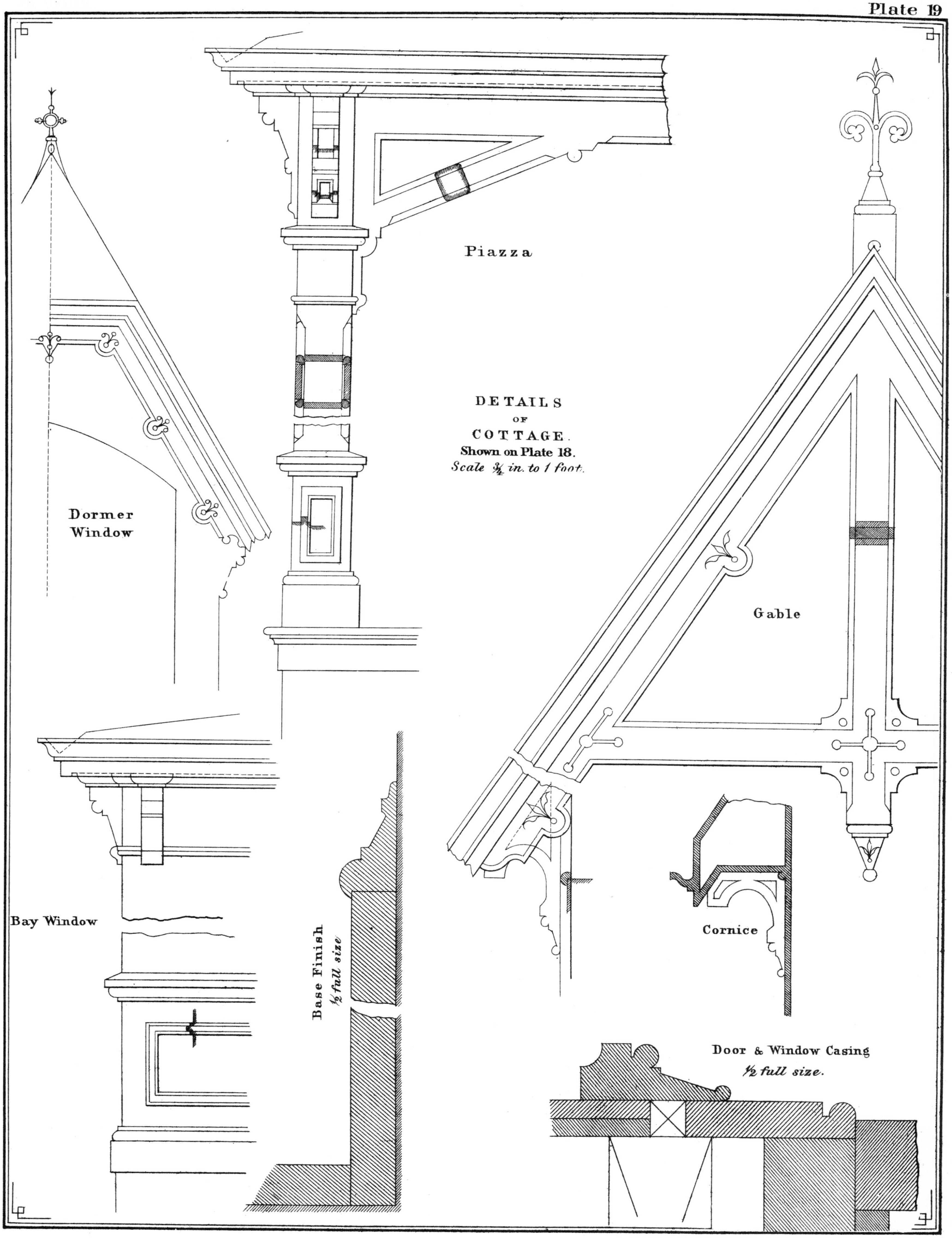

Plate 19

Piazza

Dormer
Window

DETAILS
OF
COTTAGE.
Shown on Plate 18.
Scale ¾ in. to 1 foot.

Gable

Bay Window

Base Finish
½ full size

Cornice

Door & Window Casing
½ full size.

Plate 20

Nos. 1, 2, 3. 4, 5, 6, 7, 8, 9, 10, 11, drawn to scale of 4 feet to one inch ; 12, 13, 14, 15 and 16 to scale of 2 feet to one inch.

PERMANENT WOOD FILLING,
FOR HOUSE-BUILDERS.

This article, being a very penetrating and non-evaporating anti-damp of extreme durability, is a perfect and permanent Filling for the Pores of Wood. It is designed to take the place of Lead Paint, in a measure, for all *new* work. (Where lead or zinc has been once used, it is not applicable.)

It is of two shades, dark and light, and is adapted for use on either soft or hard wood finish. On the latter, the light shade, which leaves the natural color of the wood unchanged, is commonly used. On pine, whitewood, and other soft woods, the Dark Filling is employed, and serves as a paint, turning the color of the wood to a rich brown, but allowing the grain to show through plainly.

Where it can be used, it is cheaper, quicker and better than the ordinary paint, and when once put on will last for years. It may be finished with a bright gloss, or left "dead," as the painter desires.

VALENTINE'S VARNISH FACTORY,
Corner of Ewen & Jackson Streets, Brooklyn, E. D., N. Y.,
WHERE THE PERMANENT WOOD-FILLING IS MADE.

Experience has proved that the "P. W. F." not only produces a very rich and handsome finish, but that, on account of its permanent elasticity, it will neither crack nor flake off; besides which it saves time, labor and cost, and is more convenient, cleanly and healthful than lead paint.

Send for full Descriptive Circular, setting forth the advantages of the PERMANENT WOOD FILLING on house work, describing its appearance, giving directions for use, price, etc., etc., to

VALENTINE & CO.,
88 CHAMBERS STREET, N. Y.

VENTILATORS

AND

WARM-AIR

REGISTERS

IN GREAT VARIETY, FOR

Tuttle's Patent Register.

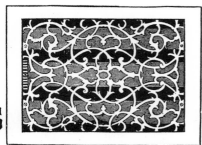

Tuttle's Patent Register.

DWELLINGS,
STORES,
CHURCHES,
PUBLIC HALLS, &c.

MANUFACTURED AND FOR SALE BY THE

TUTTLE & BAILEY MANF'G CO.

No. 83 (formerly No. 74) BEEKMAN STREET, New York.

Those about to build or re-model buildings are interested in the

𝕎arming and 𝕍entilation

of their apartments.

A good Warming Apparatus placed in the cellar of a dwelling, warming with one fire—no coal and ashes to be carried up and down stairs—is a

Ceiling Ventilator, for Churches or Halls.

luxury, and can be now obtained at a

VERY MODERATE COST.

The warmth is regulated, where it passes into the room, by an Ornamental Register, placed either in the floor or side wall.

Every Sleeping Room, Sitting Room, Dining Room, Church or Public Hall should have one or more.

VENTILATORS,

Which should, if possible, open into or be connected, *at the floor*, with a *warm ventilating flue*, affording a chance for the foul air to escape, thus inviting the fresh, warm air, to enter the apartment.

The Cooking Range and the Heater should connect with different chimneys, so that in each chimney a *Warm Ventilating Flue* can be secured.

Tile Pipe makes an excellent Chimney Flue for the Range or Heater, and when placed inside a large brick flue, will when in use, warm the flue in which it is placed, thus making a genuine *Ventilating Shaft*, into which the Ventilators should open, or be connected with, by conductors under the floors.

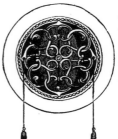

Tuttle's Patent Ventilator.

Price List and Catalogue will be sent free upon application.

TUTTLE & BAILEY MF'G CO.

No. 83 Beekman Street,

NEW YORK.

Round Register—Tuttle's Patent

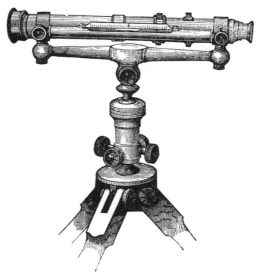

Design Patented April 25th 1871.

The above cut represents a

Design Patented by C. Graham & Son,

ARCHITECTS OF ELIZABETH, N. J.,

which may be applied to French roofs of any size or description, forming a great and acknowledged improvement in the ornamentation of French roofs—destroying the monotony of continuous slating, and presenting to the eye a beautiful, bold, and characteristic feature—particularly adapted for fronts of smaller cottages, as represented in cut.

DESIGNS FURNISHED

embodying said Patent in various designs. Also plans, specifications and working drawings for the same. Also the right to use said Patent designs on application to

C. GRAHAM & SON,

ARCHITECTS,

ELIZABETH, N. J.

ARCHITECTURAL BOOKS

PUBLISHED BY

A. J. BICKNELL & CO.,

27 Warren St., New York.

ARCHITECTURE:

By CUMMINGS & MILLER.

A PRACTICAL Book on Architectural Details; containing over 1,000 Designs and Illustrations, showing the manner of constructing Cornices, Door-ways, Porches, Windows, Verandahs, Railings, French Roofs, Observatories, Piazzas, Bay Windows, Cut Stone Work, various styles of Modern Finish, and Street Fronts of Houses, Stores, etc., etc.

One Large Quarto Volume. Price Ten Dollars.

☞ Synopsis of Contents mailed on application.

BICKNELL'S VILLAGE BUILDER:

SHOWING Elevations and Plans for Cottages, Villas, Suburban Residences, Farm-Houses, Stables and Carriage-Houses, Store Fronts, School-Houses, Churches, Court-Houses, and a Model Jail. Also, Exterior and Interior Details for Public and Private Buildings, with Approved Forms for Contracts and Specifications, containing Fifty-five Plates, drawn to scale giving the style and cost of building in different sections of the country.   Revised edition, with three additional Plates, showing designs for inside finish for Stores, Banking Houses and Insurance Offices; also, two Designs and Plans for low priced Residences; and a variety of details added to several Plates. One quarto vol. (1872). Price Ten Dollars.

☞ Full description sent on application.

VILLAGE BUILDER, AND SUPPLEMENT.

Bound in One Large Volume. Price Twelve Dollars.

LOTH'S PRACTICAL STAIR BUILDER:

A COMPLETE Treatise on the art of building Stairs and Hand-Rails. Designed for Carpenters, Builders and Stair-Builders. Illustrated with Thirty Original Plates. By C. EDWARD LOTH, Professional Stair-Builder. Illustrated Circular mailed Free.

One Large Quarto Volume, Bound in Cloth. Price Ten Dollars.

SIBLEY'S IMPROVED

LEVELING INSTRUMENT.

A want has long been felt by Carpenters, Masons, and all persons having occasion to use the ordinary spirit-level for the purpose of what is termed "running" level lines on a horizontal plane, of something less expensive than a surveyor's instrument, and more accurate than anything now in use.   In placing this instrument before the public we are sure that, for all distances within the scope of the eye, and for the practical purposes of the Mechanic and Farmer, it is equal to more expensive instruments. To the Carpenter and Mason for the purpose of leveling and squaring for foundations, to the Farmer for leveling, for ditching, and other purposes about the farm, it is indispensable.

Description and Directions for Use furnished on Application.   Price $12.

Forwarded by Express on receipt of price. The charges of transportation from New York to the purchaser are in all cases to be borne by him, we guaranteeing the safe arrival of all instruments to the extent of Express transportations, and holding the Express Companies responsible to us for all losses or damages on the way.

A. J. BICKNELL & CO., General Agents.

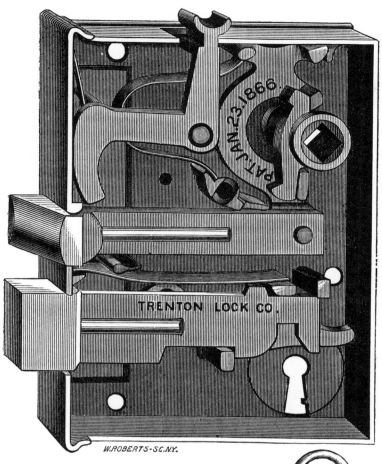
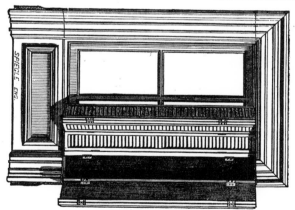

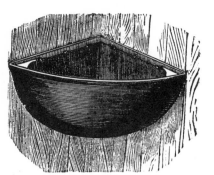

Edward Sears' Engraving Establishment

DESIGNING, PHOTOGRAPHING and ENGRAVING,

IN ALL ITS BRANCHES,

No. 48 BEEKMAN STREET, - - - - - - NEW YORK.

Having one of the largest and most complete Engraving and Designing Establishments in the United States, we beg leave to say, that we shall be happy to give Estimates for all kinds of Illustrations for Books, Periodicals, &c. Designs furnished by the best Artists, Machinery, Stores, Buildings, Catalogues of every description, Portraits, &c.

Guaranteeing satisfaction in quality, price, and prompt execution, we respectfully request your patronage.

REFERS TO

HARPER BROTHERS,
A. J. BICKNELL & CO.
D. APPLETON & CO.
D. D. T. MOORE.
PETTINGILL, BATES & CO.
CEO. P. ROWELL & CO.,
Park Row, N. Y.
AND
V. W. HARDING,
204 Chestnut St., Phila.

All kinds of Metal Work, viz. :

SOAP LABELS, CHOCOLATE, FRUIT and COLOR WORK

OF ALL DESCRIPTIONS.

American Slate Company's Emporium.

D. C. PRATT,

16 New Church Street,

Between Cortlandt and Dey,

NEW YORK,

WHOLESALE DEALER in

AND

MANUFACTURERS' AGENT for

EVERY DESCRIPTION OF

SLATE GOODS.

Marbleized Slate Mantels,
Hearths, Floor Tiles,
Bracket Shelves,
Sinks, Troughs, Wash Tubs,
Urinals, Counter Tops,
Sills, Lintels, Coping, &c.
Roofing Slate—Red,
Purple, Green and Blue,

ALL FROM THE BEST KNOWN QUARRIES.

SOLE AGENT FOR

West. Vermont Slate Co.

D. B. PROVOOST,

ARCHITECT AND SUPERINTENDENT,

No. 8 MORRIS AVENUE,

ELIZABETH, N. J.

The Harrison Bros. Color Card

COLOR NUMBER	NATIONAL BUREAU OF STANDARDS COLOR NAMES	MUNSELL NOTATION
1	Dark Green	7.5 G 3/4
3	Grayish Blue	5 PB 4/2
4	Grayish Blue	2.5 PB 5/4
5	Bluish Gray	10 B 6/1
6	Light Yellowish Green	2.5 G 7/4
7	Strong Yellowish Brown	7.5 YR 5/6
8	Dark Orange Yellow	8.5 YR 5.5/8
10	Dark Orange Yellow	7.5 YR 6/8
11	Moderate Orange Yellow	7.5 YR 7/6
12	Pale Orange Yellow	9 YR 7.5/4
13	Grayish Reddish Brown	10 R 3/2
15	Grayish Brown	7.5 YR 3/2
16	Grayish Brown	7.5 YR 4/2
17	Light Grayish Brown	7.5 YR 5/3
19	Moderate Olive Brown	2.5 Y 3/2
20	Grayish Olive	5 Y 4/2
21	Olive Gray	5 Y 4/1
22	Light Olive Brown	2.5 Y 4.5/2
23	Light Grayish Yellowish Brown	10 YR 6/2
25	Moderate Reddish Brown	7.5 R 3/6
28	Grayish Red	5 R 5/4
29	Moderate Yellowish Pink	7.5 R 7/4
31	Dark Grayish Reddish Brown	7.5 R 2/2
34	Grayish Red	7.5 R 5/2
35	Strong Reddish Brown	10 R 3/10
36	Deep Reddish Orange	7.5 R 4/12
37	Moderate Reddish Orange	1.5 YR 5/10
38	Dark Orange Yellow	7.5 YR 6.3/10
39	Brilliant Yellow	5 Y 8/10
40	Pale Greenish Yellow	10 Y 8.5/4
41	Yellowish White	5 Y 9/1
42	Deep Yellowish Green	10 GY 4/8
43	Yellowish Gray	10 Y 7.5/1
44	Yellowish White	2.5 Y 8.5/2
45	Yellowish Gray	8 YR 7/2
46	Yellowish Gray	2.5 Y 8/2
47	Grayish Yellow	3.5 Y 8/3
48	Pale Yellowish Pink	7.5 YR 8/2
49	Light Neutral Gray	N 8.0/
50	Light Bluish Green	5 BG 7.3/4
51	Grayish Reddish Brown	7.5 R 3.5/2
52	Pinkish Gray	10 R 7/1

The Harrison Bros. Color Card was matched with the Munsell Notation. The discoloration of the small chips was accounted for in matching as closely as possible these 42 colors to the Munsell System.

Frank Sagendorph Welsh, Historic Architectural Finishes Consultant
P.O. Box 214, Ardmore, Pa.   19003

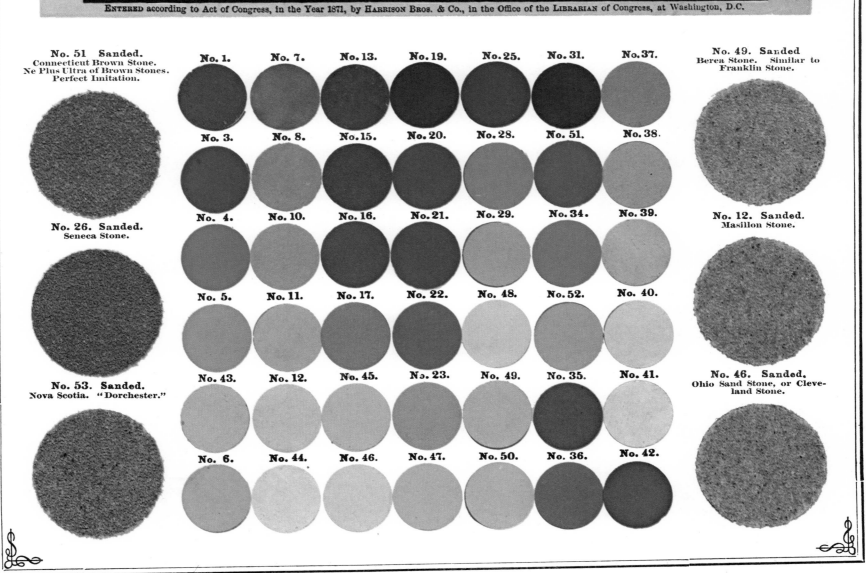

HARRISON BROS. & CO'S
TOWN AND COUNTRY

16 BURLING SLIP NEW YORK

105 SO. FRONT ST. PHILADA.

READY PREPARED PAINTS.
FOR HOMESTEAD, COTTAGE AND VILLA USE.

ENTERED according to Act of Congress, in the Year 1871, by HARRISON BROS. & CO., in the Office of the LIBRARIAN of Congress, at Washington, D.C.

No. 51 Sanded.
Connecticut Brown Stone.
Ne Plus Ultra of Brown Stones.
Perfect Imitation.

No. 49. Sanded
Berea Stone. Similar to
Franklin Stone.

No. 1. No. 7. No. 13. No. 19. No. 25. No. 31. No. 37.

No. 3. No. 8. No. 15. No. 20. No. 28. No. 51. No. 38.

No. 26. Sanded.
Seneca Stone.

No. 4. No. 10. No. 16. No. 21. No. 29. No. 34. No. 39.

No. 12. Sanded.
Masillon Stone.

No. 5. No. 11. No. 17. No. 22. No. 48. No. 52. No. 40.

No. 53. Sanded.
Nova Scotia. "Dorchester."

No. 43. No. 12. No. 45. No. 23. No. 49. No. 35. No. 41.

No. 46. Sanded.
Ohio Sand Stone, or Cleve-
land Stone.

No. 6. No. 44. No. 46. No. 47. No. 50. No. 36. No. 42.

Patterns of Minton's Tiles for Floors,

FOR SALE BY

MILLER & COATES, 279 PEARL ST., NEW YORK.

SCALE ONE INCH TO A FOOT.

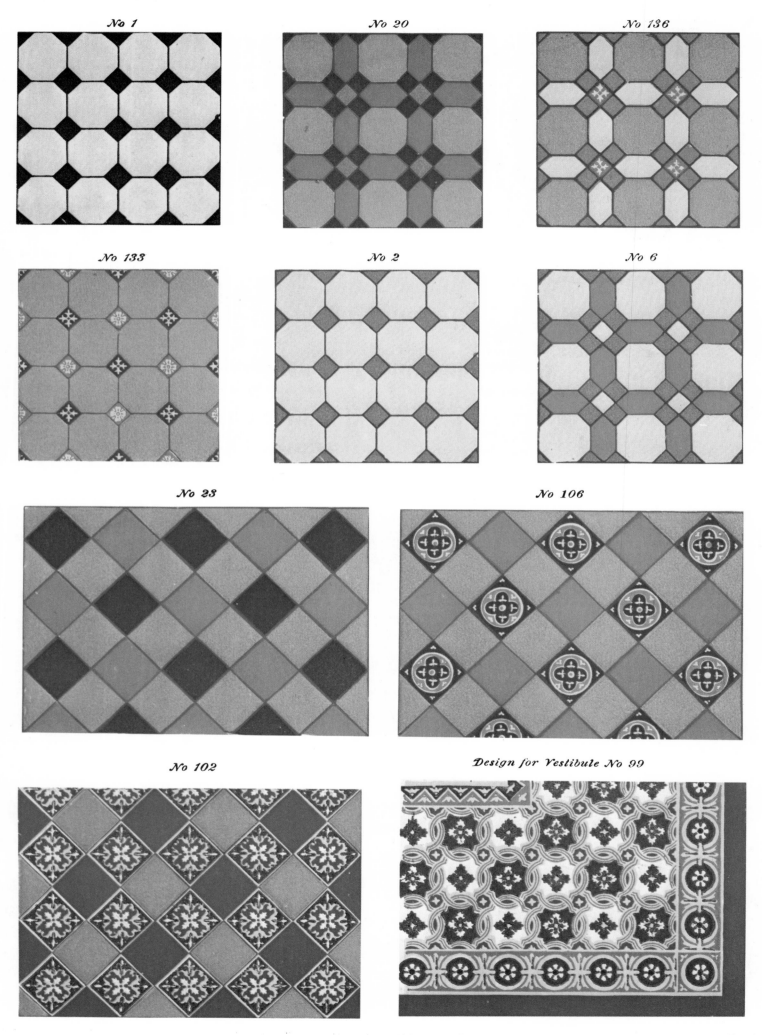

No 1   No 20   No 136

No 133   No 2   No 6

No 23   No 106

No 102   Design for Vestibule No 99

OTHER PRICES AND PATTERNS WILL BE SENT ON APPLICATION.